We don't need a feminine d[...]
does not give us one. She pres[...] [...]
both men and women so desperately need, a robust introduction
into theology that will lead the reader to adore, delight in, and
praise God for who He is and what He has done. I'm glad to
see Christian Focus call women to better theology. Stark doesn't
give us a theology for women, but a woman's voice directing us
all to the glory of God.

Aimee Byrd

Author of *Housewife Theologian*, *Theological Fitness*,
and *No Little Women*

This is an outstanding and accessible treatment of the attributes
of God. I hope it will reach a wide readership and stimulate an
interest in exploring the depths of the Christian faith.

Robert Letham

Professor of Systematic and Historical Theology,
Union School of Theology, Wales

For many years Rebecca Stark has been one of my favorite
bloggers. I'm thrilled to see her now extend her voice to books
in this brilliant little volume on the attributes of our great God.
It aptly displays so much of what I enjoy about her writing: it
is theologically astute, devotionally inspiring, and powerfully
written. I highly recommend it.

Tim Challies

Founding blogger of Challies.com
Pastor at Grace Fellowship Church, Toronto,
author of several books

We can easily say, 'Lord, I want to see your glory,' but the way we see His glory is through an understanding of what He is like, which is the focus of Rebecca Stark's book, and should be the focus of every Christian's life. With the help of the Holy Spirit, understanding who God is and what He is like is the secret to growing in Christlikeness. I'm so excited to have *The Good Portion: The Doctrine of God for Every Woman* to teach me and others to how to meditate on God. This book is going to be an excellent discipling tool.

Arlette Mbugua

Wife of Kenneth Mbugua, senior pastor of Emmanuel Baptist Church, Nairobi, Kenya.

In this vigorous yet accessible conversation about God, Rebecca Stark seeks to equip women to know their Creator more deeply. Aiming to reveal God in all His glory, this in-depth volume (and series) is a rare find amongst the plethora of publications available for ministry to women. I highly recommend this book as a tool for woman-to-woman mentoring and group discussion.

Margaret Köstenberger

Associate Professor of Theology and Director of Women's Programs, Shepherds Theological Seminary, Cary, North Carolina, author of *Jesus and the Feminists* and co-author of *Equipping for Life* and *God's Design for Man & Woman*.

THE GOOD PORTION:

God

*The Doctrine of God
for Every Woman*

REBECCA STARK

SERIES EDITOR: KERI FOLMAR

THE GOOD PORTION:

God

*The Doctrine of God
for Every Woman*

REBECCA STARK

SERIES EDITOR: KERI FOLMAR

CHRISTIAN
FOCUS

Copyright © Rebecca Stark 2018

paperback ISBN 978-1-5271-0111-1
epub ISBN 978-1-5271-0200-2
mobi ISBN 978-1-5271-0201-9

10 9 8 7 6 5 4 3 2 1

Published in 2018
by
Christian Focus Publications, Ltd.
Geanies House, Fearn,
Ross-shire, IV20 1TW, Scotland.
www.christianfocus.com

Cover design
by Pete Barnsley

Printed and bound by Bell & Bain, Glasgow

CONTENTS

Series Preface

The priest pleaded with the young woman to renounce her faith and embrace the Roman Catholic Church. Only sixteen years of age, Lady Jane Grey had been the Protestant Queen of England for nine short days. Her cousin, the staunch Catholic Queen Mary, would pardon her life if only she would recant. Instead, Jane resolutely walked to the scaffold and publicly declared:

> I pray you all, good Christian people, to bear me witness that I die a true Christian woman. I do look to be saved by no other means, but only by the mercy of God, in the blood of his only Son Jesus Christ. (Faith Cook, *Lady Jane Grey: Nine Day Queen of England*, Darlington, England: Evangelical Press, 2004 p. 198.)

Jane Grey's confidence lay in the sure hope of the resurrection for those who trust in Christ alone.

Ann Hasseltine struggled to make her decision. She loved Adoniram and was even drawn by the excitement of exploring foreign lands. But was she willing to give up all the comforts of home for the dangers of the unknown? Could she endure leaving loved ones never to meet them again in this life? Adoniram Judson was headed to India in 1811 and had asked Ann to join him as his wife. Never before had any woman left America to become a missionary to unreached people. Ann's contemplation of Jesus made the decision for her. In her diary she wrote:

> When I get near to God, and discern the excellence of the character of the Lord Jesus, and especially his power and willingness to save, I feel desirous, that the whole world should become acquainted with this Savior. I am not only willing to spend my days among the heathen, in attempting to enlighten and save them, but I find much pleasure in the prospect. Yes, I am quite willing to give up temporal comforts, and live a life of hardship and trial, if it be the will of God. (Sharon James, *My Heart in His Hands,* Durham, England: Evangelical Press, 1998 p. 38.)

Mary King stirred her pot as she contemplated Sunday's sermon. 'Cook' was a faithful, godly woman who not only prepared hearty meals for the boys at Newmarket School, but also served up 'good strong Calvinistic doctrine' to fifteen-year-old Charles Spurgeon, who credited her with teaching him his theology:

Many a time we have gone over the covenant of grace together, and talked of the personal election of the saints, their union to Christ, their final perseverance, and what vital godliness meant; and I do believe that I learnt more from her than I should have learned from any six doctors of divinity of the sort we have nowadays. (C.H. Spurgeon, *Autobiography: Volume 1 The Early Years*, Edinburgh: Banner of Truth Trust, 1962 p. 39.)

Cook dished out spiritual food as well as meat and potatoes, and Charles Spurgeon never forgot what she taught him.

A queen, a bride and a cook: they were all steeped in Christian doctrine—biblical teaching about God. These women didn't just endure theology. They relished the truths of the Christian faith. Doctrine affected their lives and overflowed to impact others.

As women in the modern world we lead busy lives. We may juggle the responsibilities of work and school and home. We wake up in the morning to dirty laundry and an inbox full of email. We go to bed at night after washing dishes, chasing deadlines and rocking babies to sleep. Sometimes life is overwhelming and sometimes it is just mundane. The God who sent His Son into the world to rescue sinners gives meaning to both the overwhelming and the mundane. He created us to enjoy knowing Him, and it is in knowing Him that we find both meaning and joy. Psalm 16:11 says, 'You make known to me the path of life; in your presence there is fullness of joy; at your right hand are pleasures forevermore.' This is why Jesus commended Mary 'who sat at the Lord's feet and listened to his teaching' (Luke 10:39). In the midst of a busy household, Mary was enjoying doctrine—Jesus' teaching about Himself and His Father. She chose 'the good portion' and couldn't tear herself away.

How do you feel about doctrine? Do you dwell on the gospel, meditate on the excellencies of Christ and discuss the doctrines of grace? Do you relish the truths of the Christian faith? This series of books on doctrine for women is an attempt to fuel your enjoyment of God by encouraging a greater knowledge of Him. It is our hope that the biblical doctrines laid out here will not only increase your head-knowledge but will be driven down into your heart, bearing fruit in your life and overflowing into the lives of others.

Keri Folmar
September 2016

Introduction

Glimpsing Glory and Giving It Back

When the two Voyager spacecraft were launched in 1977, they each carried a special phonograph record containing sounds and images of Earth—the rumble of thunder, the howling of the wind, a song of whales, greetings in fifty-five human languages, and more.[1] Twenty-seven musical recordings representing the best of

---

[1]   'What is the Golden Record?' Voyager, The Interstellar Mission, https://voyager.jpl.nasa.gov/spacecraft/goldenrec.html

the various musical cultures of the world were also selected for the record, including a Peruvian wedding song, a men's house song from New Guinea, pan pipes from the Solomon Islands, and performances of three compositions by Johann Sebastian Bach.[2]

As I write, I am listening to a recording of an orchestra performing Bach's 'Sheep May Safely Graze.' The string section is rising above the rest of the instruments, and I can feel the peace of pasturing sheep protected by their loving shepherd. In moments like this, I know why Bach is featured more often than anyone else on the Golden Record of Voyagers 1 and 2. His music gives us glimpses of glory. When it comes to composers, he is one of the best.

But I suspect Bach would have mixed feelings about being included in a collection celebrating human musical accomplishment. He signed many of his manuscripts with the letters S.D.G—initials standing for the Latin phrase *Soli Deo gloria*, which in English means 'Glory to God alone.' Bach added these three letters to his compositions to acknowledge that the gifts he used to create them came from God, so any praise for his finished work should go to God. Bach didn't create his masterpieces to show what he could do, but to show what God had done. He composed his pieces for God's honor and not his own.

Soli Deo gloria, or 'glory to God alone,' is also the last of the Five Solas, which are five phrases commonly used to summarize the Christian truths the leaders of the Protestant Reformation were trying to recover. One of the truths the Reformers emphasized was that everyone is created to glorify God. All praise should go to Him alone—especially the praise for our salvation, which, the Reformers stressed, was wholly accomplished by Him. Later

---

2   'Music From Earth' Voyager, The Interstellar Mission, https://voyager.jpl.nasa. gov/spacecraft/music.html

when the Westminster Divines put together the *Westminster Shorter Catechism*, they answered the question, 'What is the chief end of man?' like this: 'Man's chief end is to *glorify God* and to enjoy Him forever.' Humankind was not created to glory in human achievement. Rather, honoring God and delighting in Him is every man and woman's highest calling.

Bach turned all the glory for his own work back to God. Chances are, neither you nor I will ever produce a musical masterpiece, or any other kind of widely recognized masterpiece; but still, all the talents, abilities, and opportunities we have come from God. So whatever we do—whether we work hard at a job or at school, lovingly care for children, or create pieces of art— should be done for His glory and not our own (1 Cor. 10:31). If you asked me what my goal for this book is, I would have to say my first aim is to give God glory. I want the work I've done to glorify Him alone. How could I give any other answer?

Most of all, it is my desire that each reader catch a glimpse of His glory. As you read and consider God's nature and His work, I hope you will see how glorious He is and delight in Him.

But if you're going to see glory, you have to know what to look for. God's glory is something Christians talk about, but don't often define. We assume everyone knows what *glory* means—and at some level, they probably do. Still, I'll admit that even a few years ago, if you had asked me what His *glory* was, I wouldn't have been sure how to answer. But here's what I have come to understand. God's glory is His absolute perfection and His unlimited worth. It's everything that makes Him magnificent and beautiful. Since God's whole being is absolutely perfect, worthy, magnificent, and beautiful, His glory includes all that He is.

As God reveals who He is through His works, His glory is displayed in the universe. As He discloses Himself in Scripture, He is showing us His glory. And as we study Him and see more of His perfection, worth, magnificence, and beauty, we see more of His glory.

I have tried to base what I have written about God in this book on His revelation of Himself in His Word. As you read, please check the referenced Scripture passages to see if I have succeeded. (You may also need to check the context around the verse or passage to understand how it supports the statements made.) The first chapter discusses the ways we can know God, or to put it another way, it answers the question, 'How and where does God reveal His glory to us?' Chapters 2–6 explore God's triune nature and various aspects of His character. They answer the question, 'Who and what is God in Himself apart from His creation?' The last section, which includes chapters 7–9, examines His works of creation, providence and salvation, and answers the question, 'What has God done?' At the end of each chapter, you will find questions to aid your study. The answers to some of the questions are found within the chapter they follow, but others require you to use your own God-given thinking abilities to go deeper than the chapter does. I hope you will try to answer these more difficult questions, too, and not grow discouraged if the answers don't come easily. The reward for rigorous thinking about God is the greatest treasure there is—a vision of His glory.

When God reveals His glory to us, our proper response is adoration, so I also hope that as you read this book and consider who God is and what He has done, your heart will begin to worship Him. I pray that as you learn about God, you will see His glory and return glory to Him. And I pray that your desire to do everything to the glory of God will increase, so that His glory becomes your primary goal as you go about your business at work, school, or home. *Soli Deo gloria!*

Chapter 1

Knowing God

My grand-daughter is beginning to think about God. As we were chatting in my living room, she asked me, 'Where *is* God?'

How would you answer this question so a three-year-old could understand? 'He is everywhere,' I said. 'He is here in this room with us right now.' Can you guess what came next?

'Then why,' she asked, 'can't I *see* Him?'

How do you explain what it means to be a spirit to a pre-schooler? Or what it means to be omnipresent? 'God isn't like us,' I said. 'He doesn't have a body, so you can't see Him. But He's still here.'

'Is He on this side of me?' she asked, pointing to the empty spot beside her on the sofa.

'Yes,' I answered, 'and He's on the other side of you, too. He's everywhere, remember?'

'But there's no room on that side!' she objected.

God is like no one else my grand-daughter knows. Even as I struggled to explain Him in terms she could understand, she wasn't getting it. Her young mind wasn't ready for even the simplest answers to her questions. She will understand God better as she grows, and one day she may be the adult answering a child's questions about Him, but even then, her knowledge of Him will be limited. She will never understand God completely.

Babies and Geniuses

… the things that are revealed belong to us …. (Deut. 29:29)

When it comes to knowing God, we are all a bit like my grand-daughter. Our human brains are no match for the unlimited greatness of God. I'm an adult committed to studying and learning about Him, but even so, I'm like an '[infant] struggling to understand a genius ….'[1] Wouldn't most of what the genius Albert Einstein thought and said be beyond a baby's grasp? Our ability to know God is a little like this.

But as useful as the baby and genius illustration may be for giving us a picture of our limited ability to know God, a baby is actually much closer to understanding a genius than I am to

---

1   Sproul, R. C., *Truths We Confess: A Layman's Guide to the Westminster Confession of Faith,* Vol. 1, *The Triune God* (Phillipsburg, NJ: P & R Publishing 2006), 41.

understanding God. God is infinite, but I am finite. He is the Creator; I am His creature. A baby may grow up to understand Einstein, or even be the next Einstein, but I will never understand God completely. His existence is way beyond what I will ever comprehend.

Theologians say God is incomprehensible, because no human can know Him exhaustively—or, for that matter, fully understand any aspect of His being. Consider His knowledge, for instance. The psalmist describes it as 'beyond measure' (Ps. 147:5). You and everyone you know—or better yet, you and everyone who has ever lived—could all spend your entire lives learning, and if you pooled all that knowledge, it wouldn't equal God's knowledge. Not even close! Only God Himself knows everything God knows (1 Cor. 2:10–11).

Or reflect on what it means for God to be eternal. We exist in time and can't imagine any other kind of existence, so we talk about God existing in eternity past or before 'the foundation of the world,' because we can't even think or speak of eternity without using time-bound words and categories. We know our thoughts and words aren't right, but we have no better thoughts to think or more appropriate words to speak. And it's the same for everything about God. <u>Our human minds are simply too small to completely understand any of His attributes.</u> Humbling

What's more, one of the ways we learn is by categorizing. We take something we don't understand and think of similar things we're already familiar with. We draw conclusions about something unknown based on the assumption it is like the similar things we already know. My grand-daughter did this when she asked why she couldn't see God. She thought of God as a person (why not? She knows He loves her) and concluded that like every other person she knows, if He was really in the room with her, she would be able to see Him. But learning through comparison to things and people we know doesn't work with God because He is unique. 'To whom then will you compare me,' He asks, 'that I should be like him?' (Isa. 40:25; see also 40:18 and 46:5, 9). The right answer to His question is 'no one'! We can't reason our way from human categories to true knowledge of God because He is like no one else. In fact, assuming He is like the people and things He has made is a fast track to a warped view of Him.

Even in eternity when our human thinking skills will be perfected and sin will no longer distort our view of God, we will still be finite creatures with finite minds. We will see Him face to face, so we will know Him better than we do now—and everything we think will be exactly right—but we will still not know Him exhaustively. We will enjoy learning about God for all eternity, seeing more of His glory every day as we add to our knowledge throughout our endless future, yet we will never know everything about Him. He will always be too big for our human brains, and forever unlike anyone else we know.

A realistic assessment of our ability to understand God keeps us from jumping to careless conclusions about Him—or worse, presuming to know what He ought to be like. But some people go too far and conclude that because we are finite beings, we can know nothing about God for sure. What God is in Himself, they argue, is inaccessible to us, so we can't be certain of anything about Him.

Thankfully, this isn't so. As we study God, we may be 'infants trying to understand a genius,' but the genius 'is speaking to us in our own terms.'[2] Einstein, to use the previous illustration, is explaining himself in baby-talk. Our God wants us to know Him, so He condescends to speak to us in language we can understand. He adjusts His speech to our limitations and tells us

---

2   Sproul, *Truths We Confess*, 41.

who He is. We can know God because He has shown Himself to us (Rom. 1:19).

But while we can know God truly, we can never know Him exhaustively. We can understand what He has told us, but what He hasn't told us—His 'secret things'—belong to Him alone (Deut. 29:29). If God hasn't revealed it, we can't find it out.

Speaking Our Language

[T]hese things God has revealed to us through the Spirit. For the Spirit searches everything, even the depths of God. (1 Cor. 2:10)

How does God speak to us? How does He reveal Himself? He speaks, first, through His creation. He made our world; He cares for it; He directs its history. These actions show everyone that He exists, and they tell everyone something of what He is like. The sky, the psalm says, tells of God's glory and power in language we can all hear and understand (Ps. 19:1–4; see also Rom. 1:19–20). When God sends sunshine and rain to grow the farmer's crops, He is declaring His existence and His goodness (Acts 14:17). Because God revealed Himself in His creation, deep down we all know He is there. And deep down, we all know He created us and provides for us—and we ought to worship Him (Rom. 1:21, 25, 28).

What God tells us about Himself through His creation is heard by every single person every day. It's a message spoken worldwide throughout the ages, so we call it *general revelation*. As fallen people, we choose to ignore and suppress the message of general revelation (Rom. 1:18), but nevertheless, it is always there for everyone to see and hear. There is no excuse for ignorance of God's existence and greatness.

But general revelation doesn't tell us everything we need to know about God. It doesn't, for instance, reveal that He is triune. It doesn't explain His purpose for history or unfold His plan to save. To know these truths, we need more revelation with more specific information.

This is why God gave Scripture. The Holy Spirit directed the human authors of the Bible and what they wrote is God's own message to us (2 Pet. 1:21). Scripture is called *special revelation* because God gave it to specific people at specific times in history. In the Bible He tells us more about Himself, explaining His character, purpose, and work more fully. He teaches us that God is Father, Son, and Spirit. He speaks of the Father's redeeming love for His people and His plan to send the Son to redeem them. Scripture's history records the incarnation of the Son, His death for our salvation, and His resurrection. Scripture tells us more than that God exists. It also tells us God's story.

God's final revelation of Himself is Jesus Christ. 'In these last days,' writes the author of Hebrews, '[God] has spoken to us by his Son' (Heb. 1:2). In Jesus, the incarnate Son, we can actually see God—or at least those who were with Him during His life on earth could actually see God. And those of us who live afterward can see the incarnate God-revealing Son described in the New Testament. In Jesus, the glorious perfection of the invisible God became visible (John 1:14, 18).

For us, God's special revelation in Scripture and His ultimate revelation in the Son go together, because without Scripture, we would know nothing about Jesus Christ, the incarnate Son. In the Old Testament, God set the stage for Jesus Christ to be revealed, and in the New Testament, He recorded the story of His life and explained Him to us.

Since we can know nothing about God unless He tells us, His own revelation must be the source of any true knowledge of

Him. Teachers and books can guide us in our study and explain what Scripture teaches, but anything we learn about God should have its origin in what God has told us about Himself.

But to really know God, we need more than His speech to us. God has revealed Himself in creation and explained Himself in His Word, and anyone can see and read what He says. But all people naturally suppress the knowledge of God, so even though He makes Himself objectively clear, we don't see Him (Rom. 1:18, 21, 25). You might say we are blind to Him. We can't see because we don't want to see, so it's willful blindness, but still, it's real blindness. To understand God's revelation of Himself and see Him as He is, we need God's Spirit to open our 'eye[s] of faith.'[3]

From start to finish, then, true knowledge of God is His gift to us. His Spirit guided the authors of Scripture to write what we need to know. As they wrote, they were imparting the truths of God 'in words not taught by human wisdom but taught by the Spirit' (1 Cor. 2:13). And since a reader without the Spirit of God will never truly grasp or 'accept the things' found in Scripture (1 Cor. 2:14), it is also God's Spirit who causes us to understand and believe what they wrote. True knowledge of God comes through 'sanctified human reason'[4]—our own thinking ability directed by the Spirit of God—and careful study of the Bible, God's own revelation of Himself.

True Worship and Living Faith

> ... we have not ceased to pray for you, asking that you may ... walk in a manner worthy of the Lord ... increasing in the knowledge of God. (Col. 1:9–10)

---

3   Berkhof, Louis, *Systematic Theology* (Grand Rapids, MI/Cambridge, U. K.: Wm. B. Eerdmans Publishing 1996), 34.

4   Berkhof, *Systematic Theology*, 34.

Do you know the Old Testament story of the golden calf (Exod. 32:1–6)? Moses, the leader of the people of Israel, went up on Mount Sinai to receive the Ten Commandments and other instructions from God. He was gone for forty days and the people grew anxious without him, so they asked Aaron, the priest, to make gods to lead them in Moses' absence. Together with Aaron, then, they made a golden calf to worship. It's shocking how quickly they turned to polytheism and idolatry, breaking both God's first commandment—'You shall have no other gods before me' (Exod. 20:3)—and His second—'You shall not make for yourself a carved image' (Exod. 20:4).

But there's something else to note: When the Israelites made the calf, they said, 'These are your gods, O Israel, who brought you up out of the land of Egypt!' In their minds, the one golden calf was not the only god. They were, it seems, crediting the calf with working with the one true God to bring them out of Egypt. They were not necessarily denying that God brought them out of Egypt, but rather, denying that He had done it alone. And when they feasted after sacrificing to the calf, they called it 'a feast to Yahweh.' Yahweh is the true God's name, so when they celebrated, they were trying, in their twisted way, to honor the true God. And as they tried to honor Him, they got at least two details about Him right. They called Him by the right name, and they acknowledged one of His works.

But a few right ideas about God didn't keep the Israelites from idolatry. Even as they attempted to worship Him, their minds remade the one true God into a smaller, weaker god. They reimagined Him as a god who wasn't powerful enough to accomplish His will without help from other powers, and one who was willing to share His glory with an image they had crafted from their own possessions.

Their story is evidence of what the apostle Paul teaches in Romans 1: all people are naturally inclined to idolatry. With their golden calf, the Israelites exchanged 'the glory of the immortal God for images resembling mortal man and birds and animals and creeping things' (Rom. 1:23). They exchanged 'the truth about God for a lie' (Rom. 1:25). We read their story and wonder how they could have been so foolish, but worshiping a carved image alongside Yahweh didn't seem bizarre to them because believing in multiple gods and worshiping idols were normal in the cultures around them. We live in a different culture and time, and most of us aren't surrounded by idol-worshiping polytheists, so we might never build an actual golden calf to worship, but as fallen people we are prone to idolatry, too. Like the Israelites, we are naturally inclined to reimagine God as someone or something more like 'mortal man' than the glorious almighty God He is. Even though we might never fall as far and fast as they did, to the extent we view God as different from the One He has revealed Himself to be, we have also '[exchanged] the truth about God for a lie.'

Erin was a young woman I knew who liked to think of God as spontaneous (to use her word), because she thought a god who goes with the flow would be more exciting than one who planned everything ahead of time. But the true God has told us that He has a plan and He always sticks to it. When Erin imagined that He was spontaneous, she was exchanging the truth that God is always the same for the lie that He changes from moment to moment. She may have believed many accurate things about God, but this didn't keep her from building a false image of Him in her mind—and all because, like many her age, she placed a high value on living in the moment without a plan for the future. She preferred a god who was more like she was.

Like the Israelites and Erin, we have a natural inclination to see God as more like us than He is, and more like whatever the culture around us values than He is. But thankfully, the Spirit works within us to fine-tune our thoughts about God as we study His revelation of Himself. Yes, until we see Him face to face, the picture of God we hold in our minds will never be exactly right, so even our best thoughts of Him will be somewhat idolatrous, but the more we work to conform our thoughts to what He has told us about Himself, the more clearly we will see Him, and the more truly we can worship Him.

AN UNFLATTERING PORTRAIT

Knowing God is also the key to knowing ourselves. When the prophet Isaiah saw the living God, he cried out,

> Woe is me! For I am lost; for I am a man of unclean lips, and I dwell in the midst of a people of unclean lips; for my eyes have seen the King, the LORD of hosts! (Isa. 6:5)

Isaiah saw God in all His glory and knew instantly that he deserved to die. In the light of God's holiness, he saw his own unworthiness and the unworthiness of the people around him. God doesn't ordinarily reveal Himself this directly, so we are spared the sight of the depth of our sinfulness all at once. Instead, He gives us glimpses of Himself. He shows us a little of His righteousness and we see a little of our own unrighteousness. Each time we learn something new about God, or revisit a truth we already know, we get a clearer picture of how far we fall short of His perfection. We become more aware of our own unholiness as we see more of the glory of God.

If we only compare ourselves to people around us, people who are also sinners, we may think we're doing okay, or at least not much worse than anyone else. We give to charity or help a neighbor, and we're pleased with our efforts to love because we've done more than many do. But when we see the Father, who gave up His own Son in love, and the Son, who gave up His heavenly glory to become human, and then gave up His life to save sinners (Phil. 2:7–8), we know even our best attempts to love fall short and are always tainted with sinful self-interest.

The theologian John Calvin explained it like this:

> So long as we do not look beyond the earth, we are quite pleased with our own righteousness, wisdom, and virtue; we address ourselves in the most flattering terms, and seem only less than demigods. But should we once begin to raise our thoughts to God, and reflect what kind of being He is, and how absolute the perfection of that righteousness, wisdom, and virtue, to which, as a standard we are bound to be conformed, what formerly delighted us by the false show of righteousness will become polluted with the greatest iniquity; what strangely imposed upon us under the name of wisdom will disgust by its extreme folly; and what presented the appearance of virtuous energy will be condemned as the most miserable impotence.[5]

Unless we know God as He is, we cannot see ourselves as we are. And as painful as it is to see an accurate picture of ourselves, it is also necessary for true worship. True worship of God comes from a heart that sees how glorious He is, and understands its own unworthiness.

[BECOMING MORE BEAUTIFUL]

The same vision of God that shows us how sinful we are is also used by the Spirit to make us like more like Him (2 Cor. 3:18). God's own character is the pattern for our growth in holiness. We are commanded to be holy because He is holy (1 Pet. 1:15–16), to love

---

5   Calvin, John, *The Institutes of the Christian Religion* (Peabody, MA: Hendrickson Publishers, Inc. 2008), 5.

our enemies because He loves those who hate Him (Matt. 5:43–45), and to be merciful because He is merciful (Luke 6:36). And Paul reminds those who have seen the Son's humility—His willingness to give up His glory and His life for us—to pattern their lives after His by counting 'others more significant than [themselves]' and by looking 'not only to [their] own interests, but also to the interests of others' (Phil. 2:3–4).

A woman I know raised three biological children, and when they were grown, adopted three more children. Then she began caring for foster children, too. When I stayed with her recently, her home was crowded and her schedule was full as she cared for her three adopted kids, all middle schoolers, and three preschool foster children. At her age most people anticipate retirement with less work and fewer responsibilities, but she has taken on more. She continues to put the interests of children who need her care ahead of her own interests. Why does she sacrifice like this? Because she knows and loves God who sacrificed His own Son, and because she knows and loves the Son, who sacrificed His life to help people who couldn't help themselves. She is patterning herself after God's holy character. As she gives of herself to help the helpless, she is becoming more like the God she knows and loves.

This is the way it should work for every believer. We won't all exchange our retirement for a house full of children, but the pattern for our growth in holiness should be the perfection of God. Jesus commanded us to 'be perfect, as [our] heavenly Father is perfect' (Matt. 5:48), and to do this we need to know God in His perfection. We can't be like Him if we don't see Him as He is! As we study God, the Holy Spirit uses the truths we learn to change us 'from one degree of glory to another.' The more we '[behold] the glory of the Lord,' the more like Him we will grow (2 Cor. 3:18). The more we see His beauty, the more beautiful we become.

DEEPENING LOVE

The study of God keeps us from idolatry, shows us our sinfulness, and provides the knowledge of God necessary for our sanctification. But the best reason to study Him is to grow our love for Him. How do we turn the truths we learn about God into love for Him? J. I. Packer suggests meditating before God on one truth at a time. The kind of meditation Packer recommends doesn't involve emptying the mind, but focusing it. It is 'the activity of holy thought, consciously performed in the presence of God, under the eye of God, by the help of God, as a means of communion with God.'[6] When we prayerfully ponder what God reveals about Himself, we behold His glory. We can't help but see His beauty and our love for Him deepens.

Some say the study of God—or *theology*—can be a hindrance to living faith. Too much head knowledge of God, they argue, can lead to a cold heart before Him. This much of their argument is true: there are some who acquire knowledge about God, but have no true love for Him. But the root of the problem isn't knowledge. After all, don't we need to know *something* about another person before we can truly love them? Could a wife love a husband she knew nothing about? And assuming he's a man of good character, doesn't she love him more as she grows to know him better over time? It's the same with love for God. We must know about Him to love Him. Knowledge of God isn't a hindrance to living faith, but the beginning of it. Knowing too much about God isn't what causes cold hearts, but cold hearts develop when we don't follow the truths we learn back to the face of the living God.

---

6   Packer, J. I., *Knowing God* (Downers Grove, IL: InterVarsity Press 1993), 23.

The best way to prevent a cold heart is to ask God to increase our love for Him as we learn more about Him and see more of His glory. This is a request we can expect Him to answer because for us to know and love Him is exactly what He wants from us. 'I desire steadfast love and not sacrifice,' He says, 'the knowledge of God rather than burnt offerings' (Hosea 6:6). And again, '[L]et him who boasts boast in this, that he understands and knows me, that I am the Lord who practices steadfast love, justice, and righteousness in the earth. For in these things I delight, declares the Lord' (Jer. 9:24).

Are you curious about God? Like my little grand-daughter, do you want to know what He is like? I hope so, because it pleases Him when we want to know Him. He chose to reveal Himself because He wants us to behold His glory. It's one of the reasons He made us.

Prayer

Unsearchable God,

Thank you for wanting me to know you, and for revealing yourself to me in language I can understand. As I work my way through this study, will you teach me more of who you are and what you have done? As I grow in knowledge, will you show me more of your glory? And as I see more of your glory, will you increase my love for you? Will you keep my heart warm toward You as I learn more about you?

QUESTIONS

KNOWING GOD

We can know God because He has revealed Himself, first, through everything He has made, and then through His words in Scripture. His ultimate revelation of Himself is in Jesus, the incarnate Son of God.

1. Read Psalm 145:3. What does this verse teach about God? What does it say about your ability to know Him fully? Ask God to increase your wonder at His greatness as you meditate on this verse.

2. Read Jeremiah 9:23–24. What do these verses teach about God? What do they say about the value of knowing Him? Ask God to increase your desire to know Him as you meditate on these verses.

3. What are some of your unanswered questions about God? Have you looked in Scripture for answers? Or are they the kind of questions we can't answer because God hasn't revealed the answers to us?

4. Have you ever doubted Scripture's portrayal of God? Have you questioned whether God would really do the things Scripture says He did? Have you speculated about God and gone beyond what He reveals about Himself? How does a proper assessment of our ability to know God and His ability to teach us about Himself guard against these errors?

5. When Isaiah saw God, he cried, 'Woe is me! For I am lost' (Isa. 6:1–5), but when we see God face to face in all His

glory in eternity, we will rejoice to be with Him. Why will our experience of God's presence in eternity be different than Isaiah's earthly experience of His presence?

6. Does the thought of learning more about God for all of eternity give you joy? Why or why not? How does it feel to know the God of the universe wants you to know Him?

Chapter 2

He Is One and He Is Three

As a young girl I sat in the front pew of my home church during summer Bible classes while a teacher held up a poster with a drawing of a large three-leaf clover. The first clover leaf was labeled *Father*, the second was labeled *Son*, and the third was labeled *Holy Ghost*. If you were taught the Christian doctrine of the Trinity as a child, you may have seen a similar illustration—

although if you're much younger than I am, the last leaf was probably labeled Holy *Spirit* rather than Holy *Ghost*.

There is no question that the doctrine of the Trinity is difficult to explain and difficult to understand. Teachers use illustrations like sprigs of clover to try to make it simpler for children—and everyone else—to grasp. The Trinity can seem like a complicated math or logic problem, and using an analogy to show how something can be both one and three seems like good teaching strategy. But the problem with the three-leaf clover analogy is that a clover is not actually much like the Trinity. Three clover leaves join together to make one sprig of clover; each leaf is only one-third of the whole sprig. But the Father, Son, and Spirit don't join together to make the triune God. Each person of the Trinity is fully God, not one-third of God. And unlike the three clover leaves, which can be plucked from the sprig, the three persons of the Trinity, although distinct, can't be separated.

What is true for clover is also true for other illustrations of the triune God. When it comes to the Trinity, analogies tend to be more confusing than enlightening.

Consider another illustration I heard used to teach Sunday school children. The Trinity, the teacher said, is like an egg. An egg is one, but also three, since an egg consists of an eggshell, an egg yolk, and an egg white. Can you spot the issues with this illustration? It has the same problems as the sprig of clover, and one more for good measure. First, the shell, yolk and white are parts of the whole egg, but Father, Son, and Spirit are not parts of God. Second, the shell, yolk and white can be separated, but the persons of the Trinity can't. And third, the shell, yolk and white are made of different substances. The shell is solid, but the yolk and white are liquid. The yolk has fat; the white doesn't. The Father, Son, and Spirit, however, all have the same essence. The 'stuff' of the three persons is identical. An egg may be like the Trinity on a superficial level, but dig deeper and the two are nothing alike.

Perhaps you've heard someone say the Trinity is like the three states of water. Ice, liquid and steam are three different forms of water, just like the Father, Son and Spirit (so the explanation goes) are different forms of God. This analogy actually illustrates a Trinitarian heresy called *modalism* better than it does the Trinity. Modalism teaches that God is one person who shows Himself to us in three different forms or *modes*. The modes—Father, Son and Spirit—don't coexist, but exist one at a time. Ice, water and steam illustrate this false teaching perfectly. The same water can be ice when the temperature is below freezing, change to liquid when the temperature rises, and become steam when it boils. It's just like the (supposed) God of modalism, who (the modalist says) shows Himself as Father in the Old Testament, Son in the Incarnation, and Spirit at Pentecost. Someone who has learned about the triune God by comparing Him to states of water may have to unlearn a few things to come to an orthodox understanding of the Trinity.

When we try to make the doctrine of the Trinity simpler by using things in our world to illustrate it, we tend to muddle everything up instead. And isn't this what we would expect? How could there be an effective earthly illustration of a God who is like nothing in creation?

If we can't use illustrations to learn the doctrine of the Trinity, how can we learn it? We could start with the official creeds and definitions, I suppose, and learn what they say and mean. But God knows Himself better than any human teacher does, and He knows our human learning abilities better than we do. Doesn't He know the best way to explain Himself to us? The best way for us to learn about Him? Shouldn't we follow His lead, then, when we teach and learn about the Trinity? Doesn't it make sense to start a study of His triune nature by looking at how He revealed it to us?

God used both words and actions to teach His people that He is one God who exists as three persons. Scripture is our record of His words and actions, so that's where we'll start our study of the Trinity. We'll move through the Bible, first examining His revelation of Himself as the one and only God, and then His revelation of Himself as three eternal persons: Father, Son and Spirit.

Laying the Foundation

[T]he LORD is God; there is no other. (1 Kings 8:60)

God began His written revelation of Himself like this: 'In the beginning, God created the heavens and the earth' (Gen.1:1). The opening statement of the Bible tells us God's first act in history. He created everything there is—everything, that is, except God Himself, who was already there before anything or anyone else existed.

From the start of God's story, this is clear: the God who created the universe is the only God there is. He alone existed before the beginning. He is the only one who is eternal. Everything was created by Him and, as the Creator of everything, He is the ruler of everything. All of creation belongs to Him and all of creation has a duty to worship Him. There is no room for any other deity.

Throughout the Old Testament, God reinforced and extended this basic lesson. He commanded Moses to teach the people of Israel that He is the only true God. He commanded the people of Israel to continually teach these words to their children:

> Hear, O Israel: The LORD our God, the LORD is one. You shall
> love the LORD your God with all your heart and with all your
> soul and with all your might. (Deut. 6:4–5)

The people groups surrounding the Israelites worshiped many
false gods, but Israel must worship only the one true God
Yahweh—the all-capped *LORD* in these verses. Yahweh is the
only real God and His people should be completely devoted to
Him. 'You shall have no other gods before me,' He commanded
(Deut. 5:6–7). The Israelites' neighbors might be polytheists,
but they must be monotheists.

But the Israelites weren't faithful to Yahweh. They kept
returning to the polytheistic practices of their neighbors.
Remember the golden calf (Exod. 32)? This was just one of
many episodes of idol worship in their history. Yahweh had to
keep reminding them that He is the only real God, and none of
the other so-called gods actually exist. 'I am the first and I am the
last; besides me there is no god,' He said (Isa. 44:6). 'Before me
no god was formed, nor shall there be any after me' (Isa. 43:10).
And again, 'I am God, and there is no other' (Isa. 45:22; see also
verses 5–6). This *one-God-only* message is repeated so frequently
that we know one of the goals of the Old Testament is to teach
monotheism—the worship of Yahweh alone—to God's people.

Eventually, with the foundational truth of His oneness
established, God added to His story. '[W]hen the fullness of
time had come,' He sent His Son and His Spirit into the world
(Gal. 4:4–6), and in these acts, God revealed His triune nature
to humankind.[1] The New Testament is a record and explanation
of the incarnation of the Son and the outpouring of the Spirit,
so it is also the revelation of the Trinity. There are no explicit

---

1   White, James R., *The Forgotten Trinity: Recovering the heart of Christian Belief*
     (Minneapolis, MN: Bethany House Publishers 1998), 166–167.

statements of what we have come to call the doctrine of the Trinity, but the building blocks of the doctrine are there, implied in the New Testament's history and teaching.

Let's go searching, then, for the New Testament's Trinitarian building blocks. But as we find them, keep in mind that they sit on the foundational truth God established in the Old Testament: *He is one.* Even as the Son and Spirit are revealed, there is still only one God who created everything.

Disclosing More

> And now, Father, glorify me in your own presence with the glory that I had with you before the world existed. (John 17:5)

Many years ago, I lived next to a young woman who was studying to become a minister in a very liberal Protestant denomination. Sometimes our conversations turned to religious matters, and one day she told me she wasn't sure if she believed Jesus was really God. She was, she explained, 'still studying the matter.' If she had believed that Scripture was God's perfect revelation to us (unfortunately, she didn't), her study would have been a short one. There's no doubt that the gospels, the New Testament's written records of the acts and teachings of Jesus, present Him as God's equally divine incarnate Son.

What would my future minister friend have found if she had started studying the deity of Jesus with the scriptural accounts of His life? If she had begun by reading the gospel of John, she would have immediately seen his introduction of the Son in the prologue:

> In the beginning was the Word, and the Word was with God, and the Word was God. He was in the beginning with God. All things were made through him, and without him was not any thing made that was made. (John 1:1–3)

Deity:

The *Word,* who was the 'Son from the Father' (John 1:14), was 'in the beginning,' John wrote. Before the creation of the world, the Word already was. He existed eternally—and He existed eternally *with God.* '[T]he Word,' writes James White, 'was eternally face-to-face with God, that is … the Word has eternally had a relationship with God.'[2] And not only was the Word *with* God, but 'the Word *was* God.' The Son shared God's nature; all the attributes of deity belonged to Him. Everything that existed was created 'through Him,' so He wasn't a created being, but the Creator.

We can sum up John's prologue like this: The Word *was* the eternal creator God, but was also in some way eternally *with* the creator God. In this mysterious introduction, John set the stage for the rest of his gospel by hinting at truths about the Son that will become more clear as the story unfolds.

'I Am'

As he continued to recount the life of Jesus, the incarnate Son, John recorded several instances in which Jesus referred to Himself with the words 'I am' (John 6:20, 8:24, 28, 58, 18:5). In the Old Testament, the one true God told Moses His name was *I am who I am* (Exod. 3:14–15; see also Deut. 32:39; Isa. 41:4, 43:10; and more), so when Jesus used 'I am' to refer to Himself, He was declaring His deity by claiming to be the same *I Am* who appeared to Moses. His words revealed that He was the same 'LORD [or Yahweh], the God of your fathers, the God of Abraham, of Isaac, and of Jacob' (Exod. 3:15–16). And anyone familiar with the Old Testament who heard Him speak would have recognized this.

Jesus' claim to deity is especially obvious in John 8:58. Here, He told the Jewish leaders, 'Truly, truly, I say to you, before

---

2   White, James R., *The Forgotten Trinity,* 52.

Abraham was, *I am*' (emphasis mine). He claimed, first, to share God's name, *I Am*. And second, when He used the present tense *am* rather than the past tense *was* when He spoke of His existence before the time of Abraham, isn't He suggesting that His existence transcends time? But only *God* transcends time! We know the Jews understood Jesus' words to be a declaration of His deity because they immediately picked up stones to stone Him for blasphemy (John 8:59). In this 'I am' statement, Jesus announced that He was God, and the Jewish leaders knew it.

'I Can'

During His earthly ministry, Jesus also claimed to have other rights and abilities that belong only to God. When He healed the paralytic, for example, He also forgave His sins. The Jewish leaders watching and listening accused Him of blasphemy once again, because, they argued, only God can forgive sins. Jesus didn't correct them because they were right: only God can actually forgive anyone's sins. Instead, He doubled down on His claim to deity. 'The Son of Man,' He told them, 'has authority on earth to forgive sins' (Luke 5:20–24). He insisted the God-only right to forgive sins belonged to Him, too.

And when the Jews criticized Him for healing a man on the Sabbath, Jesus responded by declaring that He had the same right to work on the Sabbath as the Father. 'My Father is working until now, and I am working,' He said (John 5:16–17). The Father worked every day, Sabbaths included, to sustain the universe, yet He wasn't breaking the law against working on the Sabbath because He is the one who established the Sabbath law in the first place. He made the Sabbath and He rules over it. When Jesus stated that He, like His Father, could work on the Sabbath without breaking God's rules, He was asserting His deity, and again, the Jewish leaders understood Him perfectly. They accused Him of 'making himself equal with God,' and Jesus didn't correct them this time, either. Rather, He upped the ante by adding to the list of God-only rights and abilities that belonged to Him. He claimed to be able to give life (verse 21). He declared His right to judge people (verse 22), and His right to receive worship (verse 23). In fact, '*whatever* the Father does,' He said, the Son can do, too (verse 19, emphasis mine). With each one of these statements, Jesus asserted His full deity.

Do you see where this is going? And we've only hit a few of the highlights of the evidence from the gospels for the deity of the Son.

Sharing Glory, Love, and Honor

Later, in His final prayer before His crucifixion, Jesus asked the Father to 'glorify me in your own presence with the glory that I had with you before the world existed' (John 17:5). He also spoke of the love the Father had for Him 'before the foundation of the world' (John 17:24). According to Jesus, the Son was with the Father and loved by the Father before the world existed. We know, then, that the Son is eternal, and we also know that only God is eternal. These two statements from Jesus are unmistakable claims to deity. They also give us a glimpse of the eternal *personal* relationship between the Son and the Father. The Father loved the Son and shared His glory with Him eternally, so we know they are eternally *distinct* persons. Jesus' prayer teaches us that the Father and the Son are both God, and that they exist eternally in a personal relationship of mutual love and honor.

Finally, after His resurrection, Jesus appeared to His disciples. One disciple, Thomas, wasn't there. The other disciples reported back to Thomas: they had seen Jesus and He was alive! But Thomas was skeptical. 'Unless I see in his hands the mark of the nails, and place my finger into the mark of the nails, and place my hand into his side,' he said, 'I will never believe' (John 20:19–25).

Eight days later, the risen Jesus appeared to His disciples again, and this time Thomas was present with them. 'Put your finger here, and see my hands; and put out your hand, and place it in my side,' Jesus said to him. 'Do not disbelieve, but believe' (John 20:27).

Jesus presented Thomas with the exact evidence he demanded. The nail marks and spear hole were undeniable proof of Jesus' resurrection, and Thomas believed. 'My Lord and my God!' he exclaimed (John 20:28). When he called Jesus 'my God,' he affirmed the deity of the Son. Thomas' confession stands as one of the strongest scriptural evidences of the deity of Jesus. He addressed Jesus as *God*, and there's no getting around it. If Jesus wasn't truly God, wouldn't we expect Him to rebuke Thomas for his ardent false worship? Wouldn't He have objected to Thomas giving Him honor that belonged to God alone? But instead, Jesus called his confession an expression of true faith (John 20:29), so we know Thomas got it exactly right when he confessed that Jesus was God.

What's more, Jesus blessed all those who come to believe Jesus is truly God without seeing or touching His resurrected body (John 20:29). If you are a believer—if you believe Jesus is God—this special blessing of Jesus is for you.

These texts, along with many others from the New Testament's record of the Incarnation and earthly ministry of Jesus, leave no doubt that Jesus is the Son of God, and that as the Son of God, He is also God. There was no good reason for my old friend the prospective pastor to hold off on a commitment to the deity of Christ. The evidence is everywhere in the gospel accounts. The Son, according to the authors of the gospels and Jesus Himself, existed in eternity with the Father in a personal relationship among equals. The Son is not a lesser deity, but God equal to God the Father. The Son is God, and as the incarnate Son, Jesus is God.

But even as the gospels affirm these truths about the Son, they are building on the Old Testament's previously established foundational truth. None of these newly revealed truths overturn the monotheism already taught by God. The Son is God, and yet there is still only one true God.

Revealing the Rest

> [W]hy has Satan filled your heart to lie to the Holy Spirit …?
> You have not lied to man but to God. (Acts 5:3–4)

Imagine you were one of the disciples who followed Jesus during His earthly ministry. You would have seen and heard much of what is recorded for us in the gospels. You would have heard Jesus' own testimony to His divinity. By the time He appeared after His resurrection, you probably would have echoed Thomas' confession that Jesus was God. Along with the other disciples, you would have known that both Jesus and the Father were divine, but at the same time, you would have considered yourself a monotheist.

But what about the Holy Spirit? What would you have known about Him? The explicit revelation of the third person of the Trinity doesn't happen until after Jesus ascended to heaven and the apostles personally experienced the power of the Spirit at Pentecost. Still, during Jesus' ministry, there were hints of another person, the Spirit, who is equal to the Father and the Son.

For example, at the start of Jesus' public ministry, He was baptized, and immediately afterwards,

> the heavens were opened, and the Holy Spirit descended on him
> in bodily form, like a dove; and a voice came from heaven, 'You
> are my beloved Son; with you I am well pleased.' (Luke 3:21–22)

The voice from heaven is the Father announcing that Jesus, who had just been baptized, is 'my beloved Son.' But along with the Father and the Son there is one more person—the *Spirit,* who 'descended on [Jesus] in bodily form, like a dove.' These mysterious words don't tell me everything I'd like to know about the Spirit's presence at Jesus' baptism. If I had been there, would I have seen an actual dove, or just something dove-like coming down to Jesus? I don't know and the text doesn't say. But I do know that the Spirit was distinct from the Son because He came down *to* the Son. He was also distinct from the Father because He descended before the Father spoke from heaven. These verses describe three distinct persons present at the baptism of Jesus.

Jesus' disciples may not have been present at His baptism, but when they wrote their gospels, they told the story of it, so we know they knew what happened. If you were a disciple, what would you have made of this mysterious Holy Spirit, distinct from the Father, who descended on the Son at His baptism?

WE WILL SEND THE SPIRIT

Later, right before His crucifixion, Jesus spoke to His disciples and revealed a little more about the Spirit. The Spirit, He promised, would come from the Father to be with them after He left. Here are three excerpts from Jesus' final instructions to His disciples:

> But the Helper, the Holy Spirit, whom the Father will send
> in my name, he will teach you all things and bring to your
> remembrance all that I have said to you. (John 14:26)

> But when the Helper comes, whom I will send to you from the Father, the Spirit of truth, who proceeds from the Father, he will bear witness about me. (John 15:26)

> But when He, the Spirit of truth, comes, He will guide you into all the truth; for He will not speak on His own initiative, but whatever He hears, He will speak; and He will disclose to you what is to come. He will glorify Me, for He will take of Mine and will disclose *it* to you. (John 16:13–14, NASB)

As one of His disciples, what could you have learned about the Spirit from what Jesus said in these verses? What would you have known if you had listened carefully and understood the significance of His words? First, Jesus promised that when the Spirit came, He would teach, bear witness, guide, speak and declare things. These are all actions of a person, but not those of a mere force or power. That the Spirit does them means the Spirit is a person. Second, Jesus said the Spirit would 'declare ... the things to come,' something only God can do (see Isa. 41:22–23, 44:7). This is evidence of the deity of the Spirit. And third, Jesus said both the Father and the Son would send the Spirit. If they can send Him, then He is distinct from them. We can put these three truths together and summarize them like this: the Spirit is a person who is distinct from the Father and the Son, but who is also God.

THE ONE NAME

As Jesus prepared to ascend to heaven after His resurrection, He gave more instructions to His disciples. He commanded them to make new disciples and to baptize them 'in the name of the Father and of the Son and of the Holy Spirit' (Matt. 28:19). Notice that Jesus included the Holy Spirit in the same phrase with the Father and the Son, and more significantly, He included the Spirit with the Father and the Son in a single name. This name, Robert Letham writes, is God's '[new] covenant name in its fullness, the one name of the Father, the Son, and the Holy Spirit.'[3] The name by which the one true God's new covenant people will know Him, and the name into which they are to be baptized, is *the Father, the Son and the Holy Spirit*.

If you had been a disciple, and you heard this name, would you have concluded that the Spirit was in the same league, so to speak, as the Father and Son? Would you have thought, 'If the Father and Son are persons, isn't the Spirit also a person? If the Father and Son are both God, isn't the Spirit, too?' At least you would have been all set to understand the personhood and deity of the Spirit when He was poured out at Pentecost.

WHEN THE SPIRIT CAME

Acts, the New Testament's historical record of the work of the Spirit as He built the church, begins with more of Jesus' instructions to His disciples. He commanded them to stay in Jerusalem to wait for the Holy Spirit to empower them. He promised they would 'be baptized with the Holy Spirit not many days from now' (Acts 1:4–5), and the Spirit would give them power to be His witnesses 'in Jerusalem and in all Judea and Samaria, and to the end of the earth' (Acts 1:8). Jesus' promise was fulfilled when the Spirit came down and filled His disciples, giving them the ability to speak in foreign languages so they could tell the story of Jesus to the Jews from many nations who were gathered in Jerusalem on the day of Pentecost (Acts 2:4–11). The disciples, who had lived with the Son and worked alongside Him, now experienced the Spirit as He lived within them and gave them the ability to do the work the Son had commissioned them to do.

---

3   Letham, Robert, *The Holy Trinity: In Scripture, History, Theology, and Worship* (Phillipsburg, NJ: P & R Publishing 2004), 60.

As the Spirit continued to work, not just within the inner group of apostles, but in everyone who believed (Acts 2:38), speaking to them, giving instructions (Acts 8:29, 10:19–20, 13:2–4, 15:28, 16:6–10, 21:11), and referring to Himself as 'I' and 'me' (Acts 10:19–20, 13:2), the believers began to understand the personhood and deity of the Spirit.

The apostle Peter gave us one of the clearest statements of what the first Christians believed about the Spirit. When Ananias, one of the early believers, sold property and pretended to give all of the proceeds to the apostles even as he kept part of the money for himself, Peter accused him, first, of lying to the Holy Spirit, and then, in the next breath, of lying to God (Acts 5:3–4). Only a person can be lied to, so we know Peter understood that the Spirit was a person. And since he equated lying to the Spirit with lying to God, we also know he understood that the Spirit was God.

Putting It Together

> The grace of the Lord Jesus Christ and the love of God and the
> fellowship of the Holy Spirit be with you all. (2 Cor. 13:14)

As the Bible's historical record closed, the apostles weren't using the word *Trinity*, and they hadn't put together a formal doctrine of the Trinity, but we know from the Scripture they wrote that they believed the Father, Son, and Spirit were equally and eternally God. We also know they understood that the Father, Son and Spirit were distinct from each other, since they recorded that the Son prayed to the Father, that the Father loved the Son, and that the Father and the Son sent the Spirit. But even as they affirmed the deity of Father, Son and Spirit, and affirmed the distinctions between them, the apostles continued to insist there was only one true God (Acts 17:24–31).

A Trinitarian understanding of God undergirds everything the apostles wrote in their letters. Throughout the epistles, the authors mentioned the three persons of the Trinity together. Peter, for example, introduced his first epistle with a greeting to 'those who are elect ... according to the foreknowledge of *God the Father*, in the sanctification of the *Spirit*, for obedience to *Jesus Christ* ...' (1 Pet. 1:1–2, emphasis mine). And Paul closed 2 Corinthians with this benediction: 'The grace of the *Lord Jesus Christ* and the love of *God* and the fellowship of the *Holy Spirit* be with you all' (2 Cor. 13:14, emphasis mine). Since the New Testament authors normally used 'God' to refer to the Father, this is a Trinitarian benediction that includes Father, Son and Spirit. When the apostles mention the three persons together like this, they seem to assume the early believers reading their writings already understood that the three persons were equally divine, and that they worked together in the lives of believers.

The apostles also present salvation as a work of all three persons of the Trinity. Paul writes that 'through *him* [Christ] we both have access in one *Spirit* to the *Father*' (Eph. 2:18, emphasis mine). And again: '...it is *God* who establishes us with you in *Christ*, and has anointed us, and who has also put his seal on us and given us his *Spirit* in our hearts as a guarantee' (2 Cor. 1:21–22, emphasis mine). The author of Hebrews added that 'the blood of *Christ*, who through the eternal *Spirit* offered himself without blemish to *God*, [will purify] our conscience from dead works to serve the living God' (Heb. 9:14, emphasis mine). Our list of texts from the epistles mentioning the roles of the three persons in salvation could go on (see Gal. 4:4–7; Rom. 15:16; Eph. 4:4–6), but these three are enough to show the apostles taught that our salvation depends on the cooperative work of Father, Son and Spirit.

The Bible, Old Testament and New Testament together, presents what James White calls the 'three foundations' of the Trinity:

1. There is only one God.
2. There are three divine persons, the Father, the Son, and the Spirit.
3. These three divine persons are coequal and coeternal.[4]

These three biblical tenets are the basis for the doctrine of the Trinity as expressed in the Trinitarian creeds.

Generally speaking, the people of the ancient church believed each one of these tenets was true, although they probably wouldn't have expressed them in exactly these terms, since some of the wording is taken from later formal definitions of the Trinity. Based on God's revelation of Himself in historical acts, and His explanation of Himself in Scripture, the apostles and early Christians knew that there was only one God, and that the Father was God, the Son was God, and the Holy Spirit was God. They knew each one—Father, Son and Spirit—was personal, eternal, equal to the others in deity, and distinct from the others. They were thoroughly Trinitarian even though they didn't use the formulas for the Trinity we've come to use.

Rejecting Heresy by Definition

> In the unity of the Godhead there be three Persons of one substance.... (*Westminster Confession of Faith*, Chapter 2)

If the earliest Christians could understand the triune nature of God from their own experiences and the witness of Scripture, why would anyone need formal definitions of the doctrine of the Trinity? If they didn't need the Trinitarian creeds, why do we?

---

4   White, James R., *The Forgotten Trinity*, 26–28.

We can blame this on the heretics. The rise of heretical ideas about the nature of God and the relationships between Father, Son and Spirit forced the church to distinguish true Christian teaching about God's triune existence from false teaching. When the leaders of the church put together official statements of the doctrine of the Trinity, they were trying to wipe out these destructive heresies. The authors of the Trinitarian creeds used several terms not found in Scripture to get around the tactics of the heretical teachers. The false teachers used the language of Scripture—misinterpreted, of course—to support their heresies.[5] The men who framed the creeds worked to find language which properly represented the biblical information about God as Trinity, but which the heretics would be unwilling to affirm. Had the creeds used only biblical language, the false teachers would have happily endorsed them, and then continued to lead unwitting followers away from the truth, all the while claiming that what they were teaching was faithful to the creeds.

THE HERETIC ARIUS AND THE NICENE CREED

The Nicene Creed was drawn up in response to a fourth-century false teacher named Arius, who taught that the Son was created by the Father. The Son, he said, was the first created being and the one through whom God created everything else. As the chief agent in the creation of the universe, the Son is exalted, and even divine in some sense, but He is not God in the same way the Father is God. The Son, according to Arius, was not fully God.

There were many early theologians who opposed Arius and argued against his false teaching about the Son. Still, his teaching was accepted by most of the eastern church. The dispute between the western church, which opposed Arianism, and the eastern church, which, for the most part, affirmed it, threatened to split

---

5   Letham, Robert, *The Holy Trinity*, 2.

Christianity. Emperor Constantine called a council of church leaders to decide the issue of the nature of the Son once and for all. He hoped this would put the matter to rest and preserve the unity of the church. The council came together at Nicaea and condemned Arius' heretical teaching. The Nicene Creed, which originated in this council but was fleshed out several decades later, was a statement against Arianism.

The Nicene Creed begins like this:

> We believe in one God, the Father, the Almighty, maker of heaven and earth, of all that is seen and unseen.
>
> We believe in one Lord, Jesus Christ, the only son of God, eternally begotten of the Father, God from God, Light from Light, true God from true God, begotten, not made, of one Being with the Father ....[6]

The first words to note are 'eternally begotten.' *Eternally begotten* may seem like an oxymoron, but these words were carefully chosen to express the true distinction between the Father and the Son. That the Son is eternally begotten of the Father means He is eternally *from* the Father, not because the Father created Him, but because He was *begotten* by Him. This doesn't mean the Father gave life to the Son at some point in history, however, because the Son is *eternally* begotten. No, the Son exists eternally in a relationship of 'from-ness or begotten-ness from the Father.'[7] Or to put it another way, the Father *eternally generates* the Son. The Son never became the son of the Father, and the Father never became the father of the Son, but the Father and Son exist eternally in a relationship of father and son.

---

6   'Nicene Creed,' Theopedia, http://www.theopedia.com/nicene-creed.

7   Sanders, Fred, *The Deep Things of God: How the Trinity Changes Everything* (Wheaton, IL: Crossway 2010), 92.

The Son, to continue with the creed, is 'true God from true God.' Arius was wrong! The Son is not a lesser deity who came into being when the Father made Him, but true God—as true in His 'godness' as the Father—eternally begotten from true God.

The last phrase in the section of the creed quoted above says the Son is 'of one Being with the Father.' This is not an easy phrase to understand or explain either. What does *being* mean when it's applied to God? The best simple description of the being of God I know comes from James White. God's being, he writes, is 'the "stuff of God." It is "that which makes God, God." Because [God] is unique, His being is unique as well. Whatever the "being" of God is, creatures don't have the same thing.'[8] That the Son is 'of one being with the Father' was the specific wording in the creed that Arius' followers couldn't affirm. After all, how could a created being, which is what Arianism claimed the Son was, be of the same being (or 'stuff') as the one who created him?

THE PROCEEDING SPIRIT

The section about the Holy Spirit in the Nicene Creed isn't as detailed as the one on the Son, and this is what we would expect, since the creed was drawn up in response to a specific heresy about the nature of the Son. Here's what it says about the Spirit:

> We believe in the Holy Spirit, the Lord, the giver of life, who proceeds from the Father and the Son. Who with the Father and the Son is worshipped and glorified.[9]

First, notice that the Spirit is worshiped and glorified along with the Father and the Son. If He's worshiped with them, then He's as much God as they are. The creed clearly affirms the full deity of the Spirit.

---

8   White, James R., *The Forgotten Trinity*, 169.

9   'Nicene Creed,' Theopedia, http://www.theopedia.com/nicene-creed.

Second, according to the creed, the Spirit *proceeds* from the Father and the Son. He is eternally *from* the Father and Son, but not in the same way the Son is *from* the Father. If you're hoping for a full explanation of what it means for the Spirit to proceed, I'm afraid you won't find it here—or anywhere, for that matter. The main take-away from the use of this term to describe the way the Spirit is from the Father and the Son is that the eternal relationships between the Father, Son and Spirit are distinct. The Son relates to the Father eternally as a son, so the creed uses the term *begotten* to describe their relationship. The Spirit, on the other hand, comes from both the Father and the Son, but His relationship is not one of son to father, so the creed says He *proceeds* from them.[10]

Let's stop to sum up what the Nicene Creed teaches about the eternal relationships of the persons of the Trinity. The Son is from the Father; He is begotten of Him. The Spirit is from the Father and the Son; He proceeds from Them. And the Father is from no one. He is not begotten and He doesn't proceed.

THE ATHANASIAN CREED

The Athanasian Creed, which contains a later and more detailed definition of the Trinity than the Nicene, adds this about the Father, Son and Spirit:

> But the whole three Persons are co-eternal, and co-equal.[11]

The words *persons*, *co-eternal*, and *co-equal* are still used in definitions of the Trinity found in our Christian statements of faith, so we need to understand what they mean, too. In everyday English, we use the word *person* to refer to an individual human

---

10   For the scriptural basis for the procession of the Spirit, see John 15:26 and John 16:7.

11   'Athanasian Creed,' Christian Classics Ethereal Library, https://www.ccel.org/creeds/athanasian.creed.html.

being, but this isn't the way it's used in the formal definitions of the Trinity. The persons of the Trinity are distinct, but they aren't individuals. Each person of the Trinity is what J. I. Packer calls an 'I' in relation to two who are 'you.'[12] Each person is Himself and not the others. But He is also never separate from the others, since all three persons exist as one being.

My favorite way to explain what *person* means in the doctrine of the Trinity is to say that each person is a 'who.' The triune God, then, is one 'what'—or *being*—and three 'whos'—or *persons*.[13] (This formulation of the Trinity as one 'what' and three 'whos' is also useful for teaching children the doctrine of the Trinity without using eggs, shamrocks, water, or other illustrations that do more to confuse things than clarify them.)

When the creed says the three persons are *co-eternal*, it means the Father, Son, and Spirit have forever existed together as the one being of God. No person had a beginning; each one is eternal. That the persons are *co-equal* means the Father, Son and Spirit are each fully God, and as this creed says later, 'none is greater or less than another.'[14]

BUT AREN'T THOSE OLD CREEDS OBSOLETE?

The Trinitarian creeds and definitions were formulated to guard against false teachings about the relationships of the Father, Son and Spirit. Those who put the creeds together were focusing particularly on Arianism, and much of the phrasing is specifically intended to rule out this heresy. But the creeds also include

---

12   Packer, J. I., *Concise Theology: A Guide to Historic Christian Beliefs* (Carol Stream, IL: Tyndale House Publishers 1993), 42.

13   White, James R., *The Forgotten Trinity*, p. 27. White gives credit to Hank Hanegraaff of the Christian Research Institute for this simple way to express what the Trinitarian terms *person* and *being* mean.

14   'Athanasian Creed,' https://www.ccel.org/creeds/athanasian.creed.html.

statements denying *Modalism*, the ancient heresy mentioned in the introduction to this chapter. Modalism, if you recall, teaches that the Father, the Son, and the Spirit are not distinct persons, but are merely three ways a single-person God shows Himself at different times.

Anyone who thinks we don't need these creeds anymore because Trinitarian heresies are a thing of the past is mistaken. The Nicene and Athanasian creeds never actually eradicated heresy. Arianism, in fact, continued to grow after the Nicene Council condemned it, and forms of both Arianism and Modalism still exist. Jehovah's Witnesses, for instance, believe Jesus was created, just like the ancient Arians did. Oneness Pentecostals, along with other similar groups, are modern modalists. They teach that the Father, the Son and the Spirit are simply different manifestations of the one God, who is a single person. No one who affirms what these groups teach can affirm either of these two early creeds, so the creeds still work to identify and defend against heresy.

The creeds also continue to serve us by uniting true Christians around the truth of the Trinity. We sometimes say the Nicene Creed in services at my own church, and as we recite these ancient words together, we are joining with the long-ago Christians who wrote them, and with the Christians throughout the centuries who recited them, to affirm this basic truth of the Christian faith: the one true God exists eternally as three persons.

Adoring the Trinity

I bind unto myself today
The strong name of the Trinity,
By invocation of the same
The Three in One and One in Three.
(St Patrick's Breastplate—Cecil Alexander)

Have you come this far into this chapter on the Trinity, and even now, the picture you have of the triune God's existence as three persons in one being isn't clear? Are you thinking, 'All these definitions and I *still* don't get the Trinity'? Well, join the party! The creeds aren't meant to explain exactly how the three persons exist in the one being of God. And as we've seen, when people try too hard to explain the Trinity, they come up with illustrations that paint a clear picture, but it's not a picture of the triune God.

Like most truths about the infinite God, the doctrine of the Trinity is deep. There are things about the Trinity our finite brains can't know and our human languages can't explain. Understanding the Trinity requires work, and even then, much of what it means for our incomprehensible God to exist as three-in-one will remain beyond our human understanding.

Even so, if you are a believer, you know God as Trinity. If you are being saved, you have already experienced the triune God, because the Father, Son and Spirit are working together to save you. We'll discuss the work of the Father, Son and Spirit in salvation in more detail later, but for now, we can sum it up like this. The three persons of the Trinity exist from eternity in a relationship of mutual love. Within the eternal triune being of God, the Father loves the Son and Spirit, the Son loves the Father and the Spirit, and the Spirit loves the Father and the Son. Our triune God can be loving by nature—something that can't be said of a single-person God[15]—because He loves from eternity within Himself apart from the existence of creatures to love.

And from the overflow of love between the Father, Son and Spirit, the Father chose you in eternity and then sent His Son to die for you. In love, the Son came from the Father, lived and

---

15   Reeves, Michael, *Delighting in the Trinity: An Introduction to the Christian Faith* (Downers Grove, IL: IVP Academic 2012), 41.

died for you, and now lives in heaven interceding for you. And out of love, the Spirit came from both the Father and the Son. In love, He regenerated you and is now living in you, making you more and more like Christ. From start to finish, your salvation depends on the Trinity—Father, Son and Spirit—working together in love. Without the triune work of our loving God, you could not be saved, and neither could I.

Yes, the doctrine of the Trinity is deep, but it is also beautiful. The triune God is a God who can love deeply and save completely. Our God is perfectly glorious because He is three-in-one.

Prayer

Triune God,

Thank you for existing as Father, Son, and Spirit. I praise you, Father, for loving me and sending your Son to save me. I praise you, Son, for coming into my world to die for me. And Holy Spirit, I praise you for giving me faith, living within me, and directing my life.

When I worship you, I want to see you as the triune God you are. And I want to know the Father's love, the Son's salvation, and the Spirit's power within.

HE IS ONE AND HE IS THREE

The true God, the *Christian* God, exists as one God in three persons. We know He is triune because He has revealed Himself to us as Father, Son, and Spirit by sending the Son into our world to live as a human being, and by sending the Spirit at Pentecost to empower the apostles and then all believers. We learn of God's triune nature in Scripture, which records the incarnation of the Son and the coming of the Spirit.

1. What created things have you heard used to illustrate the Trinity? Choose one and list the ways it is *not* like the Trinity.

2. How would you teach the doctrine of the Trinity to children? At what age would you start? What would you say?

3. Is it a contradiction to say God is both one and three? Explain your answer.

4. One of the criticisms of the doctrine of the Trinity is that there is no text of Scripture that teaches it explicitly. How would you respond to this criticism?

5. Read Ephesians 1:3-14. What does it say about how the Father, Son, and Holy Spirit work together to accomplish your salvation? What does the Father do? The Son? The Holy Spirit?

6. Could a single-person God save you? Explain your answer.

7. Find a short explanation of either Arianism or Modalism and read it. Then read the Nicene creed and note the statements that exclude the heresy you chose to study. Read the Athanasian Creed and do the same. Both creeds are included at the back of the book.

Chapter 3

He Is Not Like Us

What is God? How would you answer this question? Here's what I came up with: 'God is the supreme being, the creator of the universe, and the one we worship.' I checked my work by looking up the word *God* in the *The Oxford Dictionary*. It defines a monotheistic God as 'the creator and ruler of the universe and source of all moral authority; the supreme being.'[1] It's not all that different from my definition, is it?

But the more I think about these two definitions, the less I like them. Neither actually answers the question, 'What is God?' because they both rely on the existence of the universe to define God. They define Him by His relationship to His creation, but He doesn't rely on His relationship to His creation to be what He is.

Imagine that God had chosen not to create the universe. What would He be then? It's this existence, His perfect eternal existence, that's the focus of the question 'What is God?' It is asking this: In the beginning, before God created the heavens and the earth, what was He? In the beginning, when the Word was God and the Word was with God, what was God? Or, to put it another way: What is God apart from His creation?

My definition of God didn't answer this question, and neither did the dictionary's, because they didn't go deep enough or far enough back. But the group of men who wrote the Westminster Shorter Catechism did. In the answer to the fourth question of the catechism, 'What is God?' they listed His essential qualities: 'God is a Spirit, infinite, eternal, and unchangeable, in His being, wisdom, power, holiness, justice, goodness, and truth.'[2] These are all attributes of God—and listing His attributes is the perfect answer to the question of what He is. The Westminster Larger Catechism, written by the same group of men, defines God with an even longer list of attributes, adding 'all-sufficient, ... incomprehensible, everywhere present, knowing all things, ...

---

1   'Definition of *God* in English,' English Oxford Living Dictionaries, https://en.oxforddictionaries.com/definition/god

2   Beeke, Joel R. and Sinclair B. Ferguson, eds., *Reformed Confessions Harmonized* (Grand Rapids, Michigan: Baker Books 1999), 7.

most merciful and gracious, longsuffering ....'[3] Apart from His creation, God isn't creator or ruler or the one we worship, but He *is* infinite, eternal, unchangeable, all-sufficient, and all the rest of the attributes on these lists.

As you can see from these two similar but different answers to the same question from the same group of people, there is no one official list of divine attributes. There can't be. How can any list include all the facets of God's character? How can an infinite God be reduced to a list of attributes? But since we are finite-minded creatures, we list attributes and study them one at a time. It's the best we can do. It's one way for us to understand something about our infinite and incomprehensible God.

Since there isn't—and can't be—a complete list of divine attributes, different studies of God feature different attributes, and they sometimes call similar attributes by different names. In this study, I've divided the divine attributes into two groups: God's *incommunicable* attributes—those that belong to Him alone—and His *communicable* ones—those He shares with us. This isn't the only system for classifying attributes, and it isn't perfect. God's attributes don't fit into these categories as neatly as you might think.[4] But this is the most common system for categorizing them and the one I know best.

As we explore five of God's incommunicable attributes in this chapter, we will let God's revelation of Himself take us far enough back to catch sight of His perfect existence apart from His creation. With His help, we will go deep enough to begin to answer the question, 'What is God?' We will be peering into glorious things we could not see unless He showed them to us.

---

3   Beeke and Ferguson, eds., *Reformed Confessions Harmonized*, 7.

4   None of God's attributes are shared completely with us, even the ones we call *communicable*. And since we are made in God's image, even His incommunicable attributes have slight human parallels.

God Without Parts: Simplicity

> We all believe in our hearts … that there is a single and simple spiritual being, whom we call God …. (Belgic Confession, Article 1, The Only God)

A few years ago, I chatted with a woman who believed God would never condemn anyone to eternal hell. If God had wrath—and she wasn't sure He did—it was temporary. In the end, God's attitude toward everyone would be love, because God *is* love. She kept repeating the phrase 'God *is* love,' emphasizing the 'is' as if this one little word settled everything. Her whole argument against eternal condemnation rested on the *is*-ness of God's love. If God *is* love, she reasoned, love must be His most important attribute, the one attribute that rules them all.

Understanding the *simplicity* of God guards against this error. Are you familiar with the word 'simplicity' as it's used of God? It can be a bit confusing because when theologians speak of God's simplicity, they are using the word *simple* in a technical way, and not in the way we usually use it. That God is simple doesn't mean He is easy to understand. (Nor is the doctrine of divine simplicity easy to understand!)

That God is simple means, to use the words of the of the Westminster Confession of Faith, that He is 'without … parts.' He is not a composite or compound being, but a *simple* one.[5] He is not made up of parts.

You are not simple. You were, as the psalmist says, 'knitted … together in your mother's womb.' You have a maker who formed your 'inward parts,' joined them together, and gave you

---

5   Other terms we might use instead of *simplicity*, like *unity* or *oneness*, are even more prone to misinterpretation. *Unity* and *oneness* both imply parts which are joined together to make a whole, which is exactly what the doctrine of simplicity denies.

life (Ps. 139:13). Your existence depends on the one who made you and on the parts He formed and joined together. Everything God created is made of parts—parts that are held together by His sustaining power. Nothing in creation is simple.

But God is not like you or anything else. He has no maker. His attributes are not knitted together to form His being. He is not 'made up' of His attributes, nor are His attributes added on to His being or essence to make Him what He is. No, He is identical to His attributes. He is *simple*.

God is His attributes. The woman who saw love as His ruling attribute was right about one thing: God is love (1 John 4:8). But she missed the other 'is's' of God's being. He is light (1 John 1:5) and spirit (John 4:24) and life (John 11:25) and truth (John 14:26). The biblical statements equating God with various attributes imply the simplicity of God. He *is* all of His attributes.

LOVE AND JUSTICE, TOGETHER FOREVER

Because God is simple, we know that no attribute is more or less important than the others. The woman who didn't believe in God's eternal judgment overemphasized His love and downplayed His justice. Currently, love is probably the most frequently overemphasized attribute, but there are people who overemphasize His justice too. Ruth was an elderly woman I knew whose childhood had been dominated by a father who spoke only of God's condemnation of sin. His first question to his children when he returned home from work was, 'What sins did you commit today?' He followed up with a daily lecture on the fearsome wrath of God. Ruth's father taught her that God was a God of judgment, but he neglected to teach her about His love. Sadly, as an adult, she became too terrified of committing sin to leave her own home. She lived her life focused on God's just condemnation of sin, and couldn't see the forgiveness for sinners that flows from His saving love.

But love and justice, like all of God's attributes, belong together. Christ's atoning death on the cross demonstrates the harmony between God's love and His justice. As the apostle Paul explains:

> ... God put [Christ Jesus] forward as a propitiation by his blood ... to show God's righteousness, because in his divine forbearance he had passed over former sins. It was to show his righteousness at the present time, so that he might be just and the justifier of the one who has faith in Jesus. (Rom. 3:25–26)

In His *love*, God sent His Son to die so He could forgive sin without compromising His *justice*. From His love, He executed His plan to forgive sin, not by suppressing His justice, but by showing it. He put Jesus Christ 'forward as a *propitiation*'—a sacrifice that appeased His just wrath against sin, and in this one act, we see an expression of both His justice and His love. From His love, God made a way for anyone who believes to stand before Him justified despite their many sins, and it isn't a way that ignores His wrath, but satisfies it. If only Ruth had understood this!

God's simplicity has implications for the rest of our study of His nature. First, as we've just seen, since God is simple, one attribute shouldn't be emphasized at the expense of others, or one attribute regarded as more true to His nature than others. And any thought that God can limit or set aside one of His attributes, even temporarily, is just plain wrong. When He justified sinners, God *couldn't* do it by suppressing or ignoring His justice, because all of His attributes are identical with His being. They are what He is as God. He can't limit any aspect of His being without ceasing to be God.[6]

---

6   Horton, Michael, *The Christian Faith: A Systematic Theology for Pilgrims on the Way* (Grand Rapids, Michigan: Zondervan 2011), 229-230.

Second, that <u>God is simple means He is the same being throughout history.</u> Have you ever heard someone say God was vengeful during the Old Testament times, but since Christ came, He is full of love? We know this statement isn't right because God is simple. <u>In every time period, all of His actions are consistent with all of His attributes.</u>[7]

God from Himself: Aseity

> ...nor is he served by human hands, as though he needed anything, since he himself gives to all mankind life and breath and everything. (Acts 17:25)

In lists of God's attributes, you're more likely to see *self-existence*, *self-sufficiency*, or *independence* used than *aseity*, but I think aseity is a much better term for this particular attribute. It describes it more precisely than any of the other words, so even though it's an old word and an uncommon one, I'm going to use it.

<u>Aseity</u> comes from the Latin *a se*, which means 'from or by oneself.' To say God is *a se*, means He exists from Himself. Nothing caused Him to exist, but He exists uncaused, 'by the necessity of His own Being.'[8] In other words, God depends on nothing outside Himself for His existence—and He can't not exist.

The first words of the Bible teach the aseity of God: 'In the beginning God created the heavens and the earth' (Gen. 1:1). Creation, this verse says, had a beginning when God created

---

7   Grudem, Wayne, *Systematic Theology: An Introduction to Biblical Doctrine* (Leicester, England: Inter-Varsity Press and Grand Rapids Michigan: Zondervan 1994), 180.

8   Berkhof, Louis, *Systematic Theology* (Grand Rapids, Michigan/Cambridge, U. K.: Wm. B. Eerdmans Publishing 1996), 58.

it. Everything that exists came from Him. But no one created God. He had no beginning, but He already existed before the beginning of everything. God existed eternally from Himself and by Himself.

Since God is simple, His attributes exist as a whole. Each of them, then, is *a se*. His love is *a se* love. It is not drawn from Him by anything within the object of His love (Deut. 7:7–8). It is independent 'from Himself' love. He doesn't love us because of our attractive qualities—and this is good news for us. That God's love is 'from Himself' means that when we fail at work, snap at our children, or just feel generally unlovely, God still loves us. We don't need to make a name for ourselves, have special talents, or even average abilities to draw His love to us. In fact, if you are a believer, from His *a se* love, God rescued you while you were His enemy (Rom. 5:10). He loves you because of who He is and not because of who you are. He loves you simply because from Himself, He loves.

God's knowledge is *a se* knowledge. We'll discuss the aseity of God's knowledge in more detail later, but for now, let's summarize what it means that His knowledge is from Himself. It means He never acquires knowledge from something or someone outside Himself, but all of His knowledge is from Himself and complete within Himself. Even what God knows about creation, He knows from Himself. He doesn't gain knowledge of creation's future through His foresight of what will happen in it. No, He knows what He can accomplish and what He has actually willed to accomplish, and this knowledge of Himself is the ultimate source of everything He knows about creation. Likewise, His knowledge of you doesn't come from you, but from Himself. He knew, before He formed you, the kind of person He would cause you to be and the plans He had for your life (Ps. 139:16). It's this *a se* knowledge—His knowledge of Himself and His plan—that is the true source of His knowledge about you.

God's will is *a se*, too. He planned everything in the universe from Himself, and He accomplishes His plan by Himself. Writing about God's plan for the salvation of both Jews and Gentiles, the apostle Paul asks, 'Who has been his counselor?' (Rom. 11:34). The right answer? *No one!* God devised His plan independently. And it is God Himself who 'works all things according to the counsel of his will' (Eph. 1:11), so the execution of His plan doesn't depend on anything outside of Himself either. He wills and He does from Himself.

IN A CLASS BY HIMSELF

The doctrine of God's aseity, writes J. I. Packer, 'stands as a bulwark against' the thought that God's existence is limited like ours is.[9] Consider how different our existence is from His *a se* existence. We are dependent creatures. We have nothing but what God provides. But God? He is independent; He is from Himself. He doesn't need anything from us—not our help, or worship, or love. He is not 'served by human hands, as though he needed anything, since he himself gives to all mankind life and breath and everything' (Acts 17:25). The money you give to your church? God doesn't need it. It came from Him in the first place and when you give, you are you are simply returning it to Him. He is providing for His church through the gifts He gave to you. Your labor? God doesn't need it either. He gave you the ability to work, and when you work for Him you are giving back from gifts you received from Him.

Or consider this: We live only because God gives us life (Acts 17:28). I try to eat wholesome food, and there's no

---

9   Packer, J. I., *Concise Theology: A Guide to Historic Christian Beliefs* (Carol Stream, Illinois: Tyndale House Publishers, Inc. 1993), 27.

question a nutritious diet is good for me, but no diet has life-sustaining power. God still determines the length of my life, and the second He stops giving me life, I will die. And while it's wise for us to take reasonable precautions to protect our personal safety, it is not our precautions that give us life, but God, and in the end, He will be the one who takes our life away. Our existence is always dependent on Him. But God? He 'has life in himself' (John 5:26). No one gives Him life, no one sustains His life, and no one takes His life away from Him. He has eternal independent existence.

Can you see why God's aseity puts Him in a class by Himself? When we understand His aseity, we see that He is nothing like us or anything else in creation.

The aseity of God is one reason to trust Him. Are you a believer? Then you can be sure you will live forever because the *a se* God has promised it. Nothing can stop Him from keeping His promises because He doesn't depend on anything or anyone outside Himself to carry out His will. What's more, the Son, who also has 'life in Himself' gives you eternal spiritual life from the never-ending supply of life flowing out from Him (John 5:26).

From His independent life, our *a se* God gives us our dependent lives. From His perfect love within the Trinity, God's 'from Himself' love freely overflows to us. How can we not be grateful that God, who needs nothing from us, is so generous to us?

God Unchangeable: Immutability

I the LORD do not change....*(Mal. 3:6)*

Another of God's incommunicable attributes is His *immutability*. That He is *immutable* simply means He can't change. Hebrews 6:17–18 lists two ways He is unchangeable:

So when God desired to show more convincingly to the heirs of the promise the unchangeable character of his purpose, he guaranteed it with an oath, so that by two unchangeable things, in which it is impossible for God to lie, we who have fled for refuge might have strong encouragement to hold fast to the hope set before us.

First, God's *purpose*—the plan He is accomplishing in history—is unchangeable. Our plans aren't like this, are they? We make plans, but they are never written in stone. Our plans change for many reasons—because of unforeseen circumstance, perhaps, or unpredictable feelings, or overconfidence in our abilities, to name three possibilities. When I travel by air, I plan my itinerary carefully, making sure there is enough time between my flights for me to make it from one flight to another. And if I have to go through customs, I allow time for that, too. I plan ahead when I pack to make sure I have what I need when I get where I'm going. But things don't always go according to plan. I've had to rebook a connecting flight when my first flight arrived late because of the long wait for de-icing before take-off. Once my luggage didn't arrive until twenty-four hours after I got to my destination, and I had to make do without it for a day. I plan carefully, but I still have to be ready to change my plans when circumstances don't go my way.

But God never changes His plans. Nothing is unforeseen or unpredictable to Him, and He has the power to do whatever He wants to do. Why would His plans ever change? If God purposes to do something, He will do it for sure.

Second, according to these verses, God's *oath* is unchangeable. If He swears He will do something, we can be certain He will do it because 'it is impossible for God to lie.' The unchangeable nature of His oath points us directly to His immutable character.

It is God's nature to be truthful, and since His nature can't change, He will forever speak the truth.

Scripture affirms the immutability of God's character in other places, too. James 1:13 says God can't be tempted with evil and He doesn't ever tempt anyone to do evil, either. He is unchangeably righteous, so it is impossible for Him to be tempted to sin, and it is impossible for Him to tempt anyone else to sin. And according to Isaiah 40:13–14, God can't be taught anything. He doesn't learn and He doesn't forget, so His knowledge never changes. His love is immutable, too. '[H]is steadfast love endures forever' (Ps. 107:1).

Since God is what He is completely and perfectly, we would expect His character to be immutable. How could it change? By adding something to *complete*? If it's possible for Him to change for the better, then what He is right now isn't perfect, is it? And if He were to change for the worse (don't worry, He can't!), He would stop being God.

Sometimes people misunderstand the doctrine of immutability and think it means God is detached from His creation and inactive in it. It doesn't. Yes, God's plan is unchanging, but He is always working in the world to accomplish it (Eph. 1:11). God is also personal, so as creatures made in His image, we can have genuine interaction with Him. When we cry out to Him, He hears us. If we pray, He will answer. It is true that the unchanging God doesn't have emotions like ours. He doesn't have feelings that change as He reacts to circumstances He doesn't control, but still, according to Scripture, He delights in the faith of His people (Num. 14:8), grieves over sin (Eph. 4:30), and is angry with those who are unfaithful to Him (1 Kings 11:9).

And there are those who read Scripture's stories of God's interaction with His creatures and think they teach that He changed His mind and His plan. For instance, after the Israelites worshipped the golden calf, the Lord threatened to wipe them out, but Moses begged for Him to spare them. The Lord listened to Moses' plea and, the text says, '*relented* from the disaster that he had spoken of bringing on his people' (Exod. 32:10–14). Does this mean God changed His mind? That He altered His plan? Some say it does.

But remember, when we read the story of Moses' intercession for the Israelites, we see the events through Moses' eyes. He told it the way he experienced it: he heard God's threat, then he interceded for the people, and God withheld His judgment.

As the story unfolds across the pages of the text, it may seem as though God changed His plan, but when we look at what Moses said to the Lord, we see that he actually confirmed the immutability of God and the immutability of God's plan. When he begged the Lord to spare the Israelites, Moses appealed to the unchanging nature of the oaths God takes. 'Remember Abraham, Isaac, and Israel,' he reminded God, 'to whom you swore by your own self, and said to them, 'I will multiply your offspring ... and all this land that I have promised I will give to your offspring and they shall inherit it forever' (Exod. 32:13). God had sworn by His own immutable self. He pledged to the fathers that He would give land to their descendants. Surely, Moses argued, God would not now change His mind, break His promise, and destroy their offspring instead!

Our immutable God accomplishes His unchanging plan for history through interaction with His creatures. We don't know the details of His plan, so from our creaturely perspective, it may seem that He changes His plan. But from God's perspective? He knows His eternal plan and He is always working to bring it to pass. He planned in eternity to give the promised land to the patriarch's descendants. He planned in eternity to threaten to destroy these same descendants after they sinned. From eternity, He planned for Moses to plead with Him on their behalf, and from eternity, He planned to listen to Moses and then withhold His threatened destruction. God accomplished His eternal plan by doing what He always planned to do: threaten to destroy, listen to Moses, and then withhold His judgment. Through it all, God and His plan remained the same.

OUR FOREVER HOME AND STEADFAST HOPE

When I was a child, my family moved frequently, and moving was a struggle for me. I am happiest when everything in my life stays the same. I've lived in my current house for thirty-three years, and I love this stability. My children grew up and left home, my husband passed away, but my home is still here, representing permanence in the changing circumstances of my life. But my home isn't truly permanent and unchangeable, is it? If it were, I wouldn't need home insurance!

My friend told me of a little boy she taught in a village in the far north of Canada. 'My mom,' he once said to her, 'is my *home*.' He could count on his mother to love him, care for him, and keep him safe, no matter what. Compared to everything else in his life, she represented stability and permanence. But years have passed since he made this remark. He must be grown and gone. Is his mother still living? Perhaps, but she won't live forever. She wasn't unchanging and neither was he. No human can be.

But God is. He is immutable. Because He never changes, we can trust Him. The passage from Hebrews 6 quoted at the beginning of this section says God's immutability is an encouragement for us to hold on to His promises to us, confident that He will always keep them. God doesn't change, so He doesn't change His plans or break His oaths. He can't change, so we can be sure of our promised final salvation in Christ. God can be my permanent home, and yours, too, because His unchangeable nature is 'a sure and steadfast anchor of [our souls]' (Heb. 6:19). He will not move and He will keep us with Him always. Our hope in our immutable God is rock-solid forever.

God Beyond Time: Eternality

> 'I am the Alpha and the Omega…who is and who was and who is to come ….' (Rev. 1:8)

God has always been and He will always be—or as Moses said, He is from 'everlasting to everlasting' (Ps. 90:2). We know He will exist forever because He is immortal (1 Tim. 6:16). He had no beginning and He will never stop existing.

But there's more to God's *eternal* existence than existing forever with no beginning and no end. God's own name 'I AM' suggests that in His own being, God does not experience the passage of time. When Jesus declared, '… before Abraham was, I am' (John 8:58), He implied that as God's Son, He had this kind of 'beyond time' existence, too. He used the present tense, 'I am,' to describe His existence before the time of Abraham, and with these words, He claimed a kind of existence for which the tenses of human language don't apply. And when Peter wrote that for God, 'one day is as a thousand years, and a thousand years as one day' (2 Pet. 3:8), at the least, he meant God doesn't relate to time the way we do. He exists beyond the moments of time as the one 'who is and who was and who is to come' (Rev. 1:4, 8).

God tells us more about His relationship to time in Isaiah:

> I am God, and there is none like me,
> declaring the end from the beginning
> and from ancient times things not yet done,
> saying, 'My counsel shall stand … (Isa. 46:9–10)

A God who declares the end from the beginning, who announces events that haven't happened yet and then brings them to pass, is a God who rules over time. A few chapters before these verses, God claimed to have '[called] the generations from the beginning' (Isa. 41:4). If every generation comes into existence as He calls them, isn't He bringing history—and time itself—into existence, one generation at a time? And if He creates time, sustains it, and rules over it, then He certainly can't be contained by it. Another way to express this is to say God *transcends* time.

But even as He transcends time, God is also acting in it, timing each of His actions according to His plan. He sent His Son into the world 'when the fullness of time had come' (Gal. 4:4), and gave Him up to die 'at the right time' (Rom. 5:6). Paul wrote that because God had already overlooked *past* sins, He put Christ forward as a propitiation 'at the *present* time' (Rom. 3:25–26). God determines the 'allotted periods' of the nations of the world (Acts 17:26). Empires rise and fall on His timetable. He had the time for Rome to fall marked on His calendar, and when the time came, He orchestrated Rome's end. God marked the day for you to be born on His calendar (Ps. 139:16), and when that day came—or more precisely, when He brought the day into existence—He brought you into this world, and gave you life and breath and everything (Acts 17:25).

We might say time is a tool God uses to carry out His perfect will. He works in creation to bring about the sequence of events He planned for history, and everything happens right on schedule according to His plan. He can use time to accomplish His purposes because He transcends time. He can govern history because He is eternal.

That God is eternal is yet another way He is in a class by Himself. He exists from everlasting to everlasting, but our lives are like mist, here one moment and gone the next (James 4:14).

We can't even speak of our present moment—our *now*—because before the words are spoken, the moment is past. But God? He is the eternal 'I AM.' And even though those who belong to Him will live with Him forever, our everlasting life will never be the same as His eternal life. Our never-ending future in the new heaven and new earth will continue to unfold, moment by moment, but He will always exist beyond the moments of time. We will forever be time-bound, and He will forever transcend it.

Right now, time brings us loss, decay and death. Our bodies age and remind us daily of our immortality. People we love grow old and die, and some don't even have a chance to grow old before they die. But beyond time's grasp, there is one constant: our eternal God. He is always there and He will always be there. We can be sure He will keep His promises even if they are not fulfilled in our own lifetime or the lifetimes of countless generations after us. The God who works all things for our good is not subject to time, but He controls it and uses it to bring about His perfect will. That God is eternal is one more facet of His glory. It's another reason for us to trust Him, and another reason to praise Him for who He is.

God Beyond Space: Omnipresence

Do I not fill heaven and earth? declares the LORD. (Jer. 23:24)

When my children were young, my husband and I would pack them up every summer for a trip down the Alaska highway to see their grandparents, cousins, aunts, and uncles. Before we reached civilization, we drove through 900 miles of rugged wilderness. There was a spot halfway where the highway summited a mountain range, and the valley below extended into the horizons. A thick evergreen forest filled the valley, but there were no roads, houses, or signs of human life. When we stopped the truck to look out over the landscape, we wondered if there was anyone down there. Chances are, the whole valley was empty. Still, anyone who ventured down into it would not be alone. God was already there because He is everywhere.

Psalm 139 contains a poetic description of God's *omnipresence*:

> Where shall I go from your Spirit?
> Or where shall I flee from your presence?
> If I ascend to heaven, you are there!
> If I make my bed in Sheol, you are there!
> If I take the wings of the morning
> and dwell in the uttermost parts of the sea,
> even there your hand shall lead me,
> and your right hand shall hold me. (Ps. 139:7–10)

We can't get away from God. He doesn't just see into every place, but His power—or His *hand*, to use David's figure of speech—is there. And anywhere His power is, all of God is. All of His being is present everywhere in the universe.

But at the same time, God is not contained in space. 'But will God indeed dwell on the earth?' King Solomon prayed. 'Behold, heaven and the highest heaven cannot contain you; how much less this house that I have built' (1 Kings 8:27). The universe can't hold God, not so much because it's not big enough to hold Him, but because 'big enough' doesn't apply to Him. In eternity past, before He created space, God was everything He is now, omnipresence included.[10] The universe can't contain Him because as pure spirit, He is not spatial.

Since space-bound existence is all we know, we can't expect to fully understand God's omnipresence. Charles Spurgeon's illustration of these two truths about His omnipresence—that

---

10   Grudem, *Systematic Theology*, 175.

He cannot be contained in space and that His whole being exists everywhere—helps a little. Spurgeon explained God's relationship to space like this: 'His circumference is nowhere, but His center is everywhere.'[11] God relates to space like He relates to time. He acts in every moment, yet is beyond time, and He is present in every place, yet is beyond space. God transcends time, and He also transcends space.

In his speech to the Athenians recorded in Acts, the apostle Paul said God is near to everyone because (here he quotes the poet Epimenides) 'in him we live and move and have our being' (Acts 17:28). I used to read this line and imagine that my existence in God is like a fish living and swimming and existing within the waters of a fish tank. But as I've learned more about God's omnipresence, I've come to see that a fish in an aquarium is a poor illustration of what Paul must have meant. For one, there are sides to an aquarium keeping the water the fish lives in contained, while God's being has no boundaries. Second, water is dispersed throughout a fish tank, so a fish must swim everywhere in the tank to experience all of the water he lives in. But God is not dispersed throughout space. We do not have to travel the universe to experience all of Him, because all of God is present in every single spot of the universe. And last, the fish is in the water, but the water is not in the fish. But God? He is present in every single cell of our bodies.

What was Paul getting at, then, when he said we 'live and move and have our being' in God? I've come to see it like this. The universe we live in is sustained by God's power, and it only continues to exist because He continues to uphold it. He sustains

---

11   Spurgeon, Charles, 'God's Nearness to Us,' Christian Classics Ethereal Library, http://www.ccel.org/ccel/spurgeon/sermons33.xxxvi.html. Spurgeon was paraphrasing a well-known quote from Blaise Pascal: 'Nature is an infinite sphere in which the center is everywhere, the circumference is nowhere.'

each person's life, too. We 'live and move and have our being' in Him because in every moment and every place, He gives us life, keeps us moving, and preserves our being by His power. And as He upholds us and sustains the world we live in, He is right there with us, or as Paul stated in His speech, He is 'actually not far from each one of us' (Acts 17:27).

When the Israelites built the golden calf to worship (Exod. 32), they thought God was no longer there with them, but they were wrong. Even while He was up on Mount Sinai with Moses, God was still present with them. He was there while they melted their jewelry down and formed an idol, and He was there on the mountain with Moses, telling him what was happening below. Nothing can be hidden from our omnipresent God. He saw the Israelites fall into idolatry, and He sees our sins, too. He knows the sins we hide from everyone else because He is always present with us. When we spend too much time online, He sees us. When we fret over small annoyances, He knows because He is there. When we are envious of others, God is watching. No one else may know, but He does. His omnipresence is a reason for us to fight all sin, even the sin we think is secret.

And when we do sin, we know God is there to hear our sincere confession and forgive us when we ask Him to. Because He is omnipresent, He can hear all of our prayers no matter where we are. '[H]e is present everywhere in the fullness of all that He is and all the powers that He has,' J. I. Packer writes, 'and needy souls praying to Him anywhere in the world receive the same fullness of His undivided attention.'[12] Someone alone in a desolate valley halfway down the Alaska highway? God is there, too. He is able to hear and able to rescue. A soccer mom driving a van full of teenagers on a busy five-lane freeway? God is with her, ready to help when she asks for help. God hears the

12   Packer J. I., *Concise Theology*, 35.

prayers of the missionary in Papua New Guinea, too, and holds her in His powerful hand. Our God exists everywhere. Anyone who seeks Him can find Him, and anyone who prays to Him will be heard.

If you are a believer, your omnipresent God is with you in every trial, ready to rescue you or give you courage to endure. Even when the time comes for you to die, God will be there with you (Ps. 23:4). He will not be watching you from a distance, but sitting beside you while you wait, carrying you when you go, and welcoming you when you arrive. Yes, *everywhere that you can be, your God is present there.*[13]

As we've studied these five incommunicable attributes, we've begun to expand on the answer to the question, 'What is God?' Since these are attributes God doesn't share with us, they are the most difficult ones for us to grasp. No matter how much we learn, we will always dance around the edges of what it means for God to be simple, from Himself, unchanging, eternal, and present everywhere. Still, because God has condescended to reveal these facets of His being to us, we can know enough about them to see His beauty in them. We can understand enough to see something of His glory.

Prayer

Eternal God,

You are not like me. You exist from yourself, but I exist from you. I change, and everything around me changes, but you are forever the same. You transcend time and space, while I am bound by them.

---

13   This is a paraphrase of the last line of Isaac Watt's hymn, *I Sing the Mighty Power of God,* which says, 'And everywhere that we can be, Thou, God, art present there.'

Remind me of my constant dependence on you, and your never-ending ability to hear me and help me. Stay with me forever, and bring me into your presence for all of eternity.

QUESTIONS

HE IS NOT LIKE US

God shares some of His attributes with us, but others, like His simplicity, aseity, immutability, eternality, and omnipresence, belong to Him alone. That God is simple means He is not made up of parts but is identical to His attributes. No attribute is more important than others, and He can't limit any of His attributes without ceasing to be God. God's aseity means He is from Himself. He is not dependent on anyone or anything to accomplish His will. God is also immutable; He never changes. When He promises, we can be sure He will fulfill His promise because His character and purpose are unchanging. God is eternal, too. He rules over time, so He can use time to accomplish His plans. And because He is omnipresent, He is always with us to hear us and help us.

1. How would you answer a child who asked, 'Where does God come from? Who made Him?'

2. If God does not need us, why are we significant to Him? If He needs nothing from us, why should we serve Him? **Love**

3. Since we know God doesn't change, how would you explain Genesis 6:5–7, which seems to say that God changed His mind about the people He created and then changed His plans for the world ?

4. How does knowing God will never change increase your **of his** trust in Him? **Unwavering Assurance promise**

5. The Bible tells us that believers have *eternal* life. How does the eternal life God gives believers differ from His own eternal life?

6. If God is present everywhere, how do you explain 2 Thessalonians 1:9, which says those who suffer eternal punishment in hell are 'away from the presence of the Lord'? How would you reconcile this verse with Revelation 14:10, which says the wicked are tormented 'in the presence of the Lamb'?

7. Do you ever feel that God is far away from you? What Scripture could you read to remind yourself that He is always with you?

8. List the attributes discussed in this chapter and think of one reason to thank God for each of them.

Chapter 4

He Is Wise and Powerful

Imagine you live in a country ruled by a king. In this kingdom, the king is an absolute ruler, so there is no constitution to hold him accountable. As a citizen of this country and loyal subject of its imaginary king, what personal qualities would you want your king to have? Let's start with his character. Since there are no rules to keep him in line, wouldn't you want him to be a man of outstanding character, a man whose actions are ruled by an inner sense of justice and a desire for the prosperity of those who live in his kingdom?

But wanting justice and prosperity for his subjects isn't everything. Wouldn't the best kind of king also be able to make the good results he desires actually happen? If he's going to be a successful ruler, doesn't your benevolent king also need to understand how his kingdom works? Doesn't he need to know all about his subjects and his resources? And doesn't he need to know how to use his knowledge of his kingdom, his subjects, and his resources to accomplish all the things he wants to do? To rule well, your imaginary king needs knowledge of his kingdom and wisdom to make prudent decisions concerning it.

What about power? Would you want your king to be powerful? Power in the hand of an absolute ruler sounds scary, but the king we're imagining is kind-hearted. Doesn't he need power to enact and enforce laws that support the safety and prosperity of his subjects? Doesn't he need power to protect his subjects from evil forces that rise up within his kingdom, or attack from outside it?

In this chapter, we begin to explore God's communicable attributes, the characteristics He shares with us as creatures made in His image. We're starting with His knowledge, wisdom, and power, three attributes that contribute to His rule over His creation. Our imaginary king needed human knowledge, wisdom, and power to rule his imaginary kingdom well, but a mere human king, even an imaginary one, doesn't have perfect knowledge, wisdom and power. He can't know everything, his judgment is never perfect, and his power is always limited, so he will never be able to accomplish all his objectives. But God has all the knowledge and wisdom He needs to choose a perfect plan for the universe He rules, and all the power He needs to implement it. He rules the universe perfectly with His infinite knowledge, wisdom, and power.

God Knows It All: Omniscience

> Great is our LORD … his understanding is beyond measure. (Ps. 147:5)

God has unlimited knowledge, so we say He is *omniscient* or *all-knowing*. Since *omniscience* starts with an *omni* prefix, and people can't ever be *omni* anything, it may seem like omniscience should be an incommunicable attribute. But *omni* simply means unlimited, and all of God's attributes, even the communicable ones, are unlimited. God's unlimited knowledge is a communicable attribute because He has given humankind the ability to know, too.[1] His knowledge is infinite and ours is finite, but He has knowledge, and so do we.

God's omniscience starts with His knowledge of Himself. He knows the depths of His own being (1 Cor. 2:10), and this is all we need to know to conclude that His knowledge is infinite. If God Himself is infinite, wouldn't knowledge of His depths be infinite knowledge?

First, God knows and understands all of His own thoughts (1 Cor. 2:11). His knowledge, like all of His attributes, is perfect (Job 37:16), eternal, and unchanging, so we know He never turns His attention from one thought to another or searches His memory to recover a thought. He is constantly aware of each one of them. I write lists because my finite mind can only focus on one thought at a time, and once I let go of a thought, I may never recover it unless I've written it down. If I have more than three items to buy at the grocery store, I take a list with me,

---

1 Theologians Louis Berkhof, Michael Horton, and Wayne Grudem all consider omniscience to be a communicable attribute.

because without it, I may forget the one item I need most. But God never needs lists because He never lets go of any of His thoughts. His mind is always focused on every one of them. This means that although you are only one person out of more than seven billion persons in the world, you don't need to compete for God's attention. He never turns His thoughts away from you. Right now, He is concentrating on you—and every other person, too.

Second, God knows all that He can do. He knows, for instance, that He can turn stones into children of Abraham (Matt. 3:9), although He doesn't choose to work this way. He knows that had He decided to rescue Jesus from the crowd that seized Him in Gethsemane before His crucifixion, He could have done it (Matt. 26:53). These are just two examples of an unlimited number of possible works for a God with unlimited ability—and our omniscient God knows them all. He knows everything His infinite power is able to accomplish.

Third, since He knows Himself, both His unchanging character and unlimited ability, God knows exactly what He would do in situations that won't ever happen because He hasn't planned for them to happen. Do you know the story of King Joash of Israel and his arrows (2 Kings 13:14-19)? Joash was distraught because he thought he was going to be defeated by the Syrians, so he visited the prophet Elisha to ask for help. Elisha commanded him to open a window and shoot one of his arrows into the ground, and Joash obeyed. This arrow, Elisha announced, was the 'LORD's arrow of victory, the arrow of victory over Syria! For you shall fight the Syrians in Aphek until you have made an end of them.' Joash shot one arrow into the ground, so God would bring him one victory in battle.

Then Elisha told Joash to shoot the rest of his arrows into the ground, but instead, he shot only three and stopped. 'You should have struck five or six times,' Elisha told him. 'Then you would have struck down Syria until you had made an end of it, but now you will strike down Syria only three times' (2 Kings 13:19).

According to Elisha, if Joash had obeyed perfectly, God would have given all the victories required for the armies of Israel to completely wipe out Syria. As a prophet, Elisha spoke for God, and his knowledge of how God would have acted came from God Himself. God knew what He would have done if Joash had shot five arrows instead of three. But God also knew that giving Joash complete victory is something He would never actually do because Joash would only shoot three of his arrows. To this one piece of hypothetical knowledge, we can add God's knowledge of what He would have done in every other event He could have caused, but didn't. God knows what He would do in every possible situation.

Since our human minds aren't much like God's mind, and we *do* forget things, let's review what we've learned about God's knowledge so far. God knows all His own thoughts—and there is no limit to them. He knows everything He is able to do, and there's no limit to the number of things He is able to do, either. And He knows what He would do in every situation that could happen but won't, and the number of these hypothetical actions is unlimited, too. It's mind boggling, isn't it? And there's still one more category of God's knowledge.

ALL THE DETAILS OF HIS PLAN

God knows every detail of His own all-encompassing unchangeable plan for the universe. His plan includes everything: all that has happened in the past, all that is happening right now, and all that will happen in the future. It includes every cause and every effect leading to every event in history. God knows it all. It's His knowledge of His all-inclusive plan for His creation that is the true source of His knowledge of everything that exists. He knows all about everything and everyone in the universe because He planned it all. Since His plan includes everything that exists and everything that happens, there is nothing in the universe—past, present, or future—unknown to Him.

He knows all the details of the most insignificant things. Scientists can't count all the stars in all the galaxies of the universe, but they estimate there are three hundred billion in our galaxy and 70 billion trillion in the observable universe.[2] But God '*determines* the number of the stars' (Ps. 147:4, emphasis mine), so He knows exactly how many there are, both in the observable universe and beyond. He knows this because He put them there. And He knows each star individually because He named each one of them (Ps. 147:4).

God knows what happened to the warbler fledglings that left their nest in my lilac bush last summer. Did any of them make it through the winter? I don't know, but God does. He knows the exact moment any one of the hundreds of billions of birds alive in the world[3] dies (Matt. 10:29). How does He know? While it's true that He sees each bird die, His sight is not the *source* of His knowledge of their death. Rather, way back in eternity when God made His all-encompassing plan, He planned each bird's life and death. He has known each bird in the world eternally, and He has known the circumstances of their death eternally. His plan is the root of His knowledge of the warbler fledglings, and every other bird, too.

---

2   Temming, Maria, 'How many stars are there in the universe?' July 15, 2014, Sky and Telescope, http://www.skyandtelescope.com/astronomy-resources/how-many-stars-are-there/.

3   Porzecanski, Ana Luz, 'How big is the bird population?' American Museum of Natural History, accessed June 26, 2016, http://www.amnh.org/ology/features/askascientist/question16.php.

God knows the depth of each body of water and the strength of each gust of wind. Right now, He knows how much water is in the marshy pond behind my house. Until its water mysteriously drained many years ago, it was a hidden lake with a swimming beach, and He knows how much water it had then, too. God knows all about the draining of the lake, not because He is constantly checking its water level, but because He eternally planned its water level. He knows the direction and speed of the spring breeze blowing through my window and across my face, not because He is measuring the wind, but because He eternally planned this moment, wind direction and speed included. Even in the most remote places on earth, God knows every puddle, every cloud, every raindrop, and every lightning strike (Job 28:24-27) because He planned them all.

Yes, these truths about God's knowledge are difficult to grasp. When we try to understand them, we are stretching our finite minds as far as they will go and still catching only glimpses of the glory of His infinite mind.

No Hiding from God

God's detailed knowledge of the universe includes every aspect of each person's life. In Psalm 139, David listed a few of the many things God knew about him personally:

> O Lord, you have searched me and known me!
> You know when I sit down and when I rise up;
>   you discern my thoughts from afar.
> You search out my path and my lying down
>   and are acquainted with all my ways.
> Even before a word is on my tongue,
> behold, O Lord, you know it altogether. (Ps. 139:1–4)

God knew what David did, thought, and said—and He knows each one of us in the same way. When you sit down for an afternoon cup of tea, God knows it. When you get up to go about your business again, He knows this, too. He knows what you are thinking right now as you read. He knows every word you speak, and He knows it before you even think to speak it.

And there's more. David goes on—

> My frame was not hidden from you,
> when I was being made in secret,
> intricately woven in the depths of the earth.
> Your eyes saw my unformed substance;
> in your book were written, every one of them,
> the days that were formed for me,
> when as yet there was none of them. (Ps. 139:15–16)

God knew David before he was born, and He knew you before you were born. God is the one who knitted you together as you grew in your mother's womb (verse 13). He knows everything about you because He made you. While you were still 'unformed substance,' He already knew every day of your life, and He knew them the same way He knows all the other details of the universe: He knew them because He planned them (verse 16). The origin of His knowledge of what you are doing right now is the plan He made in eternity.

David contemplated all the things God knew about him and responded with these words of praise—

> How precious to me are your thoughts, O God!
> How vast is the sum of them!
> If I would count them, they are more than the sand.
> (Ps. 139:17–18)

When you multiply God's complete knowledge of David by every person past, present, and future, it is indeed 'too wonderful for [us]' (Ps. 139:6). God's knowledge, David writes, is so high we 'cannot attain it' (Ps. 139:6)—and when he says this he doesn't mean that we can't have as much knowledge as God does (we can't, of course), but that we can't even begin to comprehend the extent of His knowledge.

Since God knows everything we think, do, and say, we can't fool Him. We may be able to fool other people, and even ourselves, but He knows what we are *really* like. He knows all the ugly thoughts we never speak. He knows our selfish motives, even when we hide them from ourselves. If we're wise, we'll follow David's example and ask God to search our hearts to find any 'grievous way' (Ps. 139:23–24), so we can acknowledge our sin, ask God's forgiveness, and seek His help to overcome it. And since God knows everything about us, we can trust Him to finish His work of salvation within us. He knows where we need to change and He knows how to change us. He knows all of our circumstances and has the power to work within them to conform us 'to the image of His Son' (Rom. 8:28–29).

We started this section on God's omniscience with God's knowledge of Himself. Did you notice we didn't move beyond it? God knows Himself: His thoughts, what He can do, what He would do, and His own all-encompassing plan. What else is there? What could He possibly know that wouldn't fit into one of these categories? Is there any information that could come from His creation or His creatures that wasn't already in the plan He made before creation or creatures existed? At the bottom of all of God's knowledge is God Himself, who knows everything *from Himself*. As Michael Horton writes, 'God depends on the world no more for His knowledge than for His being.'[4] This is the only way it can be. If God is from Himself, His knowledge must be from Himself.

Remember our make-believe king? The one who needed to know what was going on in his kingdom in order to rule it well? Since he's a *human* imaginary king, he can only know his kingdom as he observes and learns from it. But God's knowledge is fundamentally different from any human knowledge. Our independent God never takes in knowledge. He doesn't know about the people and things in His universe because He observes them and learns about them, or because He foresees what they will do. He knows about them because He planned for them to be what they are and do what they do. God's unlimited knowledge all originates with Him. His knowledge, like all of His attributes, is in a class by itself. God can rule the universe perfectly, because, for one, He has eternal perfect knowledge of everything.

Are you troubled by an uncertain future? Are there things you wish you could know because you think knowing more might put your mind at ease? Let your mind rest in this: God knows everything you don't know, and not merely because He sees into the future, but because He planned the future. You are in the hands of the one for whom nothing future is uncertain, the one who knows it all because He planned it all. And as we shall see, His plan is perfect.

God Achieves His Goals: Wisdom

How unsearchable are his judgments and how inscrutable his ways! (Rom. 11:33)

---

4   Horton, Michael, *The Christian Faith: A Systematic Theology for Pilgrims on the Way* (Grand Rapids, Michigan: Zondervan 2011), 259-260.

We imagined that our make-believe king was wise—but exactly what does this mean? Biblical *wisdom*, writes J. I. Packer, is 'the power to see, and the inclination to choose, the best and highest goal, together with the surest means of attaining it.'[5] If we define wisdom biblically, then we gave our king the ability to choose 'the best and highest' goals for his rule, and the ability to choose the best ways to actually accomplish them.

In real life, we are under God's rule, and He has infinite wisdom. His eternal decisions about His goals and the best ways to achieve them are perfect. He rules the universe, and as He works to achieve His purpose in it, He always succeeds.

God's wisdom and human wisdom may be defined similarly, but God's wisdom is still essentially different than human wisdom. As finite beings, we expect to grow in wisdom as we mature. As our children begin to transition into adulthood, for instance, we expect their goals to change. We hope they leave behind childish priorities, like fun and popularity, for more grown-up ones, like a useful degree, or a meaningful job, or a stable family. And we hope that with time and experience, they will learn how to achieve their more mature goals.

We also expect to make better decisions when we follow the advice of those whose judgment is better than ours. Not long ago, I accepted the counsel of a friend who suggested I drop the comprehensive insurance on my car. He argued that my car is too old and worth too little to justify the higher premiums for the additional insurance. He was right, and I grew in my understanding of the purpose of auto insurance and became wiser about the use of money by listening to his counsel.

But unlike me—and every other human being—God never grows in wisdom. His wisdom is perfect just as it is. He doesn't gain wisdom from life experience or from the counsel of others

---

5   Packer, J. I., *Knowing God* (Downers Grove, Illinois: InterVarsity Press 1993), 90.

(Isa. 40:13; Rom. 11:34). He is already infinitely wise—eternally, unchangeably, and from Himself. Wisdom never flows *to* God, but always *from* Him. He is the only source of true wisdom, so any wisdom we have, and any wisdom we receive, comes ultimately from Him.

SUNLIGHT VERSUS SHINING WORMS

God's wisdom, like all of His attributes, is incomprehensible to us. His plan and the means He uses to accomplish it are, to use the apostle Paul's words, 'unsearchable' and 'inscrutable' (Rom. 11:33). No one can completely understand His wise purpose for the universe. Even so, we can know the broad outline of His plan because He has explained it to us in Scripture. God's overarching purpose is His own glory (Rom. 11:36; Eph. 1:12)[6]—and how could it be anything else, if perfect wisdom chooses the best and highest goal? God decided to achieve this purpose by creating, sustaining, and redeeming the universe.

And His plan is working perfectly. Creation is fulfilling its purpose by showing God's glory (Ps. 19:1). His redemptive work is accomplishing His purpose, too, because as He redeems His people, and then all of creation, He will be glorified. (Eph. 1:6, 12, 14; Phil. 2:10; 2 Thess. 1:11–12; see also John 15:8, Eph. 3:10, and Rev. 19:1–8). All of God's plan—what He revealed to us and what He keeps secret—comes from His perfect wisdom, so every detail is working to achieve His purpose. Because He is wise, we know that everything that has happened, is happening, and will happen, ultimately glorifies Him.

When we are puzzled by what is happening in our lives, in the lives of those around us, in our country, or in the world, we can rest in the knowledge that through it all, God is unfolding

---

6   See the texts referenced in the next paragraph as well, and also Psalm 46:10; Isaiah 42:8; and Isaiah 48:11.

His wise plan. When our trials multiply, and we feel as if we can't catch a break, we can still be sure God knows what He is doing. When we see people in power make troubling decisions, we can be certain that in His infinite wisdom, God is accomplishing His perfect purpose in the most effective way.

When in our human wisdom we doubt the wisdom of God's plan, it's *our* judgment, not God's, that can't be trusted. '[T]here is more difference between the reason of man and the wisdom of God,' the Puritan Stephen Charnock wrote, 'than between the light of the sun and the feeble shining of the glow worms.'[7] With our glow-worm-quality wisdom we are in no position to pass judgment on what God, with His better-than-sunlight wisdom, is doing. He is always working wisely in everything, sometimes using means that make no sense to us, but perfect sense to Him, the only One with perfect wisdom.

Since wisdom is a communicable attribute, God can share it with us. We can ask Him for wisdom to handle troubling events that happen in the world, or trials that come into our lives, and know He will generously provide it (James 1:2–5). And we can grow in wisdom by studying and obeying our God-given source of wisdom, God's Word (Ps. 19:7).

God Does What He Wants: Omnipotence

Great is our LORD, and abundant in power .... (Ps. 147:5)

When I was a child, I thought of God as something like a superhero, only better. I imagined Him using His powers—or *super*powers—to fight against evil forces in the universe. But my childish picture of God wasn't much like the real one. He doesn't have superpowers, or even ultra-superpowers; He has

---

7   Charnock, Stephen, *The Existence and Attributes of God* (Lafayette, Indiana: Sovereign Grace Publishers 2001), 274.

infinite power. Nothing, not even the most powerful evil forces in the universe, can keep Him from doing everything He wants to do. There are no near misses or risky rescues with God. No other-worldly mineral or freak accident can decrease His power. He never needs His superhero friends to rescue Him, but He always accomplishes all of His plans by His own eternal unlimited power.

When the psalmist writes that God 'does all that he pleases' (Ps. 115:3), and when the apostle Paul says He 'works all things according to the counsel of his will' (Eph. 1:11), they are describing God's *omnipotence*. His omnipotence is the fuel behind His sovereignty. He has absolute rule over everything by His endless might.

Everyone knows something about His power just by living in the world He created. God's eternal power, Paul wrote, '[has] been clearly perceived, ever since the creation of the world, in the things that have been made' (Rom. 1:20). Have you seen rocky glacier-topped mountains rising out of a blue-green sea? Or yellow prairie spreading from one cloudless horizon to the other? Have you viewed the night sky with its glowing planets and glittering stars—and maybe an aurora thrown in for good measure? If you have, you've seen proof of the unlimited power of God. With His power, God created the whole universe, and now He maintains it 'by the word of his power' (Heb. 1:3). In the beginning of time, His powerful word called the world into existence, and in each moment of time, His powerful word calls for the world to keep on existing. God's power rotates the earth, revolves the moon, and keeps the sun shining. It holds every atom in the universe together, and every cell in your body, too. Paul insisted that deep down, we all know there is an almighty God because we have seen His power at work in creation. Those who deny this, he wrote, are deceiving themselves (Rom. 1:18).

ROCKS TOO HEAVY AND OTHER IMPOSSIBILITIES

You may have heard this trick question: *Can God make a rock too heavy for Him to lift?* Either answer, yes or no, is an admission that there's something God can't do, and—supposedly—a denial of the omnipotence of God. But omnipotence is not the ability to do anything at all, but simply unlimited power. An omnipotent God can put any rock He makes anywhere He wants at any time, because He has unlimited power. No rock can ever be too big for Him to lift, so making a rock too heavy to lift is one thing an all-powerful God can't do. That He can't do it is exactly what we would expect if He is omnipotent.

There are many other things an omnipotent God can't do. He can't act contrary to His nature, so He can't lie (Heb. 6:18). He can't be unjust (Gen. 18:25). He can't do what's logically impossible, either, so He can't make a three-sided rectangle. We could go on (Can He stop existing? Can He forget you?), but nothing on our list of things God can't do would actually conflict with His omnipotence.

God's omnipotence, then, is not the power to do anything at all, but the power to do everything He wills to do. There are, as we've seen, many things He can't do, either because they are logically impossible, or because they go against His nature. There are also many things He could do, like raising up children of Abraham from stones (Matt. 3:9), but doesn't choose to do. God uses His unlimited power, not to do everything He is able to do, but to do everything that He in His wisdom has chosen to do. Because He is omnipotent He has the ability to carry out His plan and accomplish His purpose.

Human beings have power, too—not infinite power, of course, but finite power that reflects God's infinite power in some ways. Omnipotence, then, is another of the *omni* attributes that is communicable. God uses His power to accomplish

His purposes, and we use our physical and mental powers to accomplish our purposes. Do you plan projects and then complete them? Have you planned a meal for family and friends and then prepared it and served it to them? As you use your human abilities to accomplish your goals, you are reflecting the power of God. Our power is finite, so we can't do everything we want to do, but we can carry out plans with our power. God's power fuels His dominion over the universe, and our God-given and God-reflecting power fuels our God-mandated dominion over creation. We rule the world as His representatives using the power He is sharing with us from His never-ending supply.

Everyone who believes experiences God's power personally. The same powerful word that called light out of darkness when the world was created 'called [us] out of darkness and into his marvelous light' (1 Pet. 2:9). We were under Satan's rule until God's power energized us and made us alive together with Christ (Eph. 2:2–6; see also 1:19–20). We have become new people through the re-creative power of God.

His power is also sanctifying those who believe. Our omnipotent God is working within us to change our desires and actions so we do what pleases Him (Phil. 2:12–13). We are becoming more righteous as His power makes us more like Christ. And His power will preserve our faith until the end and ensure our final salvation (1 Pet. 1:5). The unlimited power that created the universe and now sustains it, that raised Christ from the dead, and that works all things according to God's plan, protects the believer forever. We can trust God to save us because He is omnipotent.

Our sovereign God is infinitely more glorious than any human king could be. No human king, not even our imaginary one, will ever have a perfect purpose. No human king will ever accomplish his purpose completely. But our omniscient, wise, and omnipotent God does. With His infinite knowledge, wisdom, and power, He rules the universe, and as He rules, He accomplishes His purpose: everything He does reveals His glory. And as His glory is revealed, those who belong to Him prosper because He shares His glory with them. God rescues sinners and makes them like Himself—He changes them 'from one degree of glory to another' (2 Cor. 3:18)—all to the praise of His glory.

Prayer

All-wise and powerful God,

Thank you for the world I live in, which came from your wise purpose and was created by your power. Thank you for planning my life and giving me life. Thank you for ruling the universe with your knowledge, wisdom and power.

Show me your glory as you work in everything to accomplish your perfect plan. Direct my life with your knowledge and wisdom, and use your power to make me more like you.

QUESTIONS

HE IS WISE AND POWERFUL

God's knowledge, wisdom, and power are three attributes that contribute to His rule over His creation. He knows Himself—what He can do, what He would do in every possible circumstance, and everything He will actually do. He knows all about His creation and what happens in it because He knows His all-inclusive plan. In His wisdom God planned for everything He created to bring Him glory, and with His power He accomplishes this goal.

1. Read Psalm 139:1–18. List the things God knows about you. How does His detailed knowledge of your life benefit you?

2. Why isn't God's foresight—His ability to look into the future and see what will happen—the source of His knowledge of the future?

3. What is your goal in life? How does your personal goal fit with God's ultimate purpose for history?

4. Have you experienced trials in the past? Can you look back and see how they made you more like Christ? How they brought glory to God?

5. Are you experiencing trials right now? Do you trust that God is wise to purposefully allow them? Do you trust that they are working to make you more like Christ? That they are bringing God glory?

6. Can you add anything to this chapter's list of things God can't do? Why doesn't His inability to do these things prove He is not omnipotent?

7. How do you use your power to fulfill God's command for us to exercise dominion over creation as His representatives? How is your power like God's power? How is it different?

8. Does knowing God has infinite power make you more sure that He will accomplish your salvation? Does it increase your confidence that 'he who has begun a good work in you will bring it to completion' (Phil. 1:6)?

Chapter 5

He Is Holy

Let me tell you about the afternoon I began to understand that I was a sinner. When I was five, I spent a few hours playing at the home of a friend. We set up a pretend restaurant on the back of a flat bed trailer in her driveway. We took make-believe orders and made make-believe food for make-believe customers. When I returned home, my mother asked me about my time away. Had

I had fun? What had we done? Instead of telling the truth, I made up an elaborate story about another activity we had supposedly done. As I began to spin my tale, I felt my face flush. I knew what I was saying wasn't the truth, but instead of stopping to correct myself, I doubled down and continued to tell my made-up story with its made-up details, all the while wishing I could disappear. I'd already learned enough in Sunday school to know God doesn't approve of lying. With this little lie I caught a glimpse of my own unholiness. The shame I felt was distressing enough that more than fifty years later, I still remember it. In fact, this incident is my first full memory of my childhood.

The Holy God calls His children to holiness. 'I am the Lord your God,' He said to the Israelites. '[B]e holy, for I am holy' (Lev. 11:44; see also 19:2; 20:7; 21:8). The apostle Peter repeated God's holiness command in the New Testament. 'As he who called you is holy,' he wrote, 'you also be holy in all your conduct' (1 Pet. 1:14–16). Those who belong to God should be holy like He is.

But what does it mean to be holy—first for God, and then for His children? What is *holiness*? We'll begin to answer these questions as we explore God's *moral attributes*—His holiness and other attributes closely associated with it.

God Is Set Apart: Holiness

> Holy, holy, holy is the LORD of hosts; the whole earth is full of his glory! (Isa. 6:3)

Several years ago, I wrote a series of blog posts on the attributes of God. I included one piece on holiness, and began it by saying that of all God's attributes, holiness was the most difficult for me to define. I reread this post recently and realized I'd missed something crucial: There are two distinct meanings to the word *holy* as used in the Bible to describe God. Reading now, I can see that the old piece was confused (and confusing), and at the heart of it all was my failure to distinguish these two different meanings of holiness.

The basic meaning of the word *holy* is 'separate,' and in each of the two biblical definitions of holiness, God is separate from something. He is set apart, in the first instance, from us, His creatures, by the 'infinite distance and difference that there is between Him and ourselves.'[1] Do you remember Hannah, the barren woman in 1 Samuel who prayed for a son and then promised God that if He granted her request, she would give her son back to Him? When God gave her a son, Hannah praised Him, and in her prayer of praise she used the word *holy* this first way. 'There is none holy like the Lord,' she said. '[T]here is none besides you; there is no rock like our God' (1 Sam. 2:2). Hannah understood that no one else is holy like the one God is holy. He is the only one with the power to grow new life in a barren womb (1 Sam. 2:5). He is above us and beyond us in a class all by Himself. He is the infinite Creator who gives life, and we are finite creatures who receive the life He gives. He is *holy*!

Defined this way, holiness isn't a communicable attribute. God can't share this one-of-a-kind holiness with us because by definition it's every way we aren't (and can't be) like Him—or more precisely, it's every way He is not like us. Only God can be holy in this first sense of the word. Scripture helps us understand this kind of holiness by linking it to God's majesty and glory. Once the people of Israel had finally escaped from their Egyptian captors, they celebrated by singing a song that included these words:

---

1   Packer, J. I., *18 Words: The Most Important Words You Will Ever Know* (Ross-shire, Scotland, UK: Christian Focus Publications 2007), 165.

> Who is like you, O LORD, among the gods?
> Who is like you, *majestic* in holiness,
> awesome in *glorious* deeds, doing wonders? (Exod. 15:11)

According to this verse, in His holiness, God is not like anyone else, including the so-called gods of the surrounding nations. He is set apart, far above everyone else, 'majestic' in His holiness. His holiness is revealed in the 'glorious deeds' He does. All the wonders God works are a public display of His holiness.

The theologian Louis Berkhof calls this first kind of holiness God's '*majesty-holiness.*'[2] Majesty-holiness is not so much a distinct attribute as a general description of God. We can think of it as His deity or, as J. I. Packer suggests, His 'God-ness.'[3] God's majesty-holiness includes everything that sets Him apart as the one and only God, everything that puts Him in a class by Himself above everyone else.

The proper response to the majesty-holiness of God is worship. We worship God alone because He alone has the infinite qualities of deity. He is the only Holy One.

SEPARATE FROM SIN

The second way the Bible uses the word *holy* to describe God points to His separation from sin. He is morally pure; there is no hint of sin in Him. John the apostle refers to this kind of holiness when he writes, 'God is light, and in him is no darkness at all' (1 John 1:5). When Isaiah saw the moral purity of the Lord he cried:

---

2   Berkhof, Louis, *Systematic Theology* (Grand Rapids, Michigan/Cambridge, U.K.: Wm. B. Eerdmans Publishing 1996), 73. (Others call God's majesty-holiness His *transcendence.*)

3   Packer, *18 Words*, 165.

> Woe is me! For I am lost; for I am a man of unclean lips, and I
> dwell in the midst of a people of unclean lips; for my eyes have
> seen the King, the Lord of hosts! (Isa. 6:5).

The sight of God's *ethical holiness*—another term from Louis Berkhof[4]—highlighted Isaiah's sinfulness. When he saw God's holiness, he couldn't help but see that he deserved God's judgment. When I lied to my mother as a little girl, I felt the disapproval of the holy God, too. God's *ethical holiness* separates Him from sin, but it also separates Him from us, five-year-olds included, because in His holiness He can't tolerate any sin (Hab. 1:13)—and we are all sinners.

Unlike God's majesty holiness, His ethical holiness is a communicable attribute. This is the kind of holiness God calls for when He commands us to be holy as He is holy. We are exhorted to strive for ethical holiness because without it, 'no one will see the Lord' (Heb. 12:14). But since God is the only one who is morally pure *from Himself*, the holy conduct He demands from us doesn't have its source in us, but in Him. He shares His holiness with us by working within us to make us holy. The same passage in Hebrews that tells us to strive for holiness also teaches us that God disciplines believers so that they 'may share his holiness' (Heb. 12:10). Our holy God disciplines His children to make them holy as He is holy.

God Does What Is Right: Righteousness and Justice

> [A]ll his ways are justice.... [J]ust and upright is he. (Deut. 32:4)

We can think of *justice* and *righteousness* as two different biblical names for the same attribute of God. Our English translations use both words to translate a single word group in each of the

---

4   Berkhof, *Systematic Theology*, 74.

biblical languages—the Hebrew of the Old Testament and the Greek of the New. And in both Hebrew and Greek, the words translated *righteousness* and *justice* in our English translations carry the idea of conforming to a moral standard.[5] A righteous or just person lives up to the proper moral standard, and the proper moral standard for human creatures is the one their Creator sets for them. God gives the rules for human righteousness.

But what about God? What is the moral standard that He lives up to in order to be righteous? Who gives Him rules to follow?

If you think no one can set standards for God, you are exactly right. He has no creator; He has no ruler. No one tells Him what to do to be righteous. He doesn't conform to an outside standard of ethics to be righteous, but He is righteous by nature. His own character is His moral standard. He meets the standard of perfect righteousness by being Himself. His code of ethics, if we can call it this, is His own unchanging moral perfection.

God's righteousness and His ethical holiness are different names for what is essentially the same attribute. God is righteous; He is morally pure; He is unchangeably holy—all three statements say the same thing.

God is righteous by nature, so everything He does is righteous. He can't act unjustly or unrighteously. This doesn't mean His actions always seem just to us. A couple I know lost two sons and a baby grandson in three separate tragic incidents, all in less than three years. They were faithful to God, but received one heart-breaking loss after another from His hand. It's natural for us to wonder how circumstances like this square with the justice of God. In Psalm 73, the psalmist Asaph asked why 'the wicked' were 'always at ease,' growing richer and richer, while 'all the

---

5   Grudem, Wayne, *Systematic Theology: An Introduction to Biblical Doctrine* (Leicester, England: Inter-Varsity Press and Grand Rapids Michigan: Zondervan 1994), 203.

day long I have been stricken and rebuked every morning,' even though 'I kept my heart clean' (Ps. 73:12–14). It's when he recalled the final destiny of the wicked, and the judgment they will receive in the end, that Asaph understood that God is always just even when, from our earthly viewpoint, it may not seem like it. The faithful couple who suffered so much in this life will spend eternity in the presence of God. In the end, our just God will set everything right .

When what God is doing confuses us, we can calm our troubled minds with this truth: 'Righteousness and justice are the foundation of his throne' (Ps. 97:2). God is never unjust and He rules everyone in righteousness. As mere creatures, we are in no position to question the rightness of our Creator's actions (Rom. 9:19–20). We have no standing to judge Him, no right to 'put [him] in the wrong' (Job 40:8). But we can be confident that even when we can't understand why He does what He does, He is acting righteously. He is the perfect 'judge of the earth' (Gen. 18:25), and as He rules over us, He is never tyrannical or capricious, but always completely just. He does what is right.

Righteous Rule

In human governments, separate arms of the government usually carry out different legal functions. Some government officials enact laws, some judge lawbreakers, and some carry out legal sentences for offenders. But in God's government, He fulfills all three roles. No one else is suited for any of these duties because no one else is perfectly just.

In God's rule, He enacts the laws. He sets the standards for human righteousness and teaches the standards to us. The laws He gives are not arbitrary, but perfect reflections of His own righteous character. 'Righteous are you, O Lord,' the psalmist wrote, 'and right are your rules' (Ps. 119:137). God's rules teach His image bearers how to reflect His holiness. His laws show us how to be righteous like He is. He 'instructs sinners in the way' and leads them 'in what is right' because He is '[g]ood and upright' (Ps. 25:8–9).

The rules God gives are called *precepts*, *laws*, *commandments*, *statutes*, and *judgments*—and there are probably other biblical terms I've left out. Where do we find His rules? They are revealed most clearly in Scripture, but even those who have never read or heard God's word have instinctive knowledge of them. He has written His righteous standards for human behavior on our hearts and consciences (Rom. 2:15). Deep down, we all know how we ought to conduct ourselves.

But even though everyone knows something of God's standards, everyone rebels against them. As fallen people, we prefer to be our own bosses and write our own rules. We wish God would lower His standards a little, or better yet, do away with them altogether. But how can He relax His rules? Can He approve of sin (Hab. 1:13)? God can't change His laws because His holy character is unchanging. The problem with God's laws is not with the laws, but with us. Humanity fell, and since then, no one lives up to His standards. No one follows His rules. Since the fall, we are all lawbreakers (Rom. 3:23).

This brings us to God's second role as righteous ruler of His creation: He is the one who judges all lawbreakers. Remember, God knows everything about us, so He has a unique ability to judge us fairly for not living up to the standards He has given. He knows everything we do and every thought we think, so His verdicts are always right. God never '[clears] the guilty' (Nahum 1:3), but He always imposes the perfect sentence for every one of our sins.

Does it sometimes seem that God is ignoring wrongdoing? Asaph thought so when he complained in Psalm 73 that wicked people continued to prosper. It's true that God overlooks sin, but only temporarily. He isn't ignoring sin, but keeping a record of it. He withholds His judgment for a while, but eventually, every sin will receive the sentence it deserves, because God 'has fixed a day on which He will judge the world in righteousness' (Acts 17:31).

Finally, as the righteous judge of the earth, God executes the sentences He has imposed. He carries them out by expressing His wrath against offenders. The outpouring of God's wrath is one aspect of His activity as righteous ruler that we might prefer not to think about, but if we want to know God as He is, we need to consider His wrath.

WRATH REVEALED

Does acting from *wrath* seem beneath a righteous God? Some people argue that it is. I suspect that many who feel this way equate God's wrath with human anger, which is often unpredictable and uncontrolled. But the wrath of God isn't like human anger. He isn't like the father who tolerates his children's boisterous play on most days, but yells at them if they are loud when he's tired and has a headache. No, God's wrath is consistent; His wrath is measured. And it's the right response to human sin. 'God is only angry where anger is called for,' writes J. I. Packer. 'Even among humans, there is such a thing as *righteous* indignation, though it is, perhaps, rarely found. But all God's indignation is righteous.'[6] God's wrath isn't beneath His righteousness. It is an *expression* of it.

Justice demands that God respond to every sin with holy wrath. If He didn't, He wouldn't be true to His morally perfect

---

6   Packer, J. I., *Knowing God* (Downers Grove, Illinois: InterVarsity Press 1993), 151.

character. If God didn't have wrath against sin, He wouldn't be righteous—or to put it another way, *He wouldn't be God*.

Many years ago, a woman beloved in my small community was murdered by her estranged husband. During the husband's trial for murder, his lawyers argued that he had been enraged by a remark she made and couldn't control himself. The jury bought this defense and found him guilty of manslaughter instead of murder. And then the judge, for reasons no one could understand, ignored the prosecutor's recommended sentence of twelve years and sentenced him to only five years in prison instead.

Can you imagine how furious this woman's family was? Everyone who knew and loved her was angry, first, that her husband had been allowed to argue that he was less culpable for her murder because she (supposedly) provoked him, and second, that he received such a light sentence for the lesser crime he was convicted of. Discussions of the situation—and there were many in the months that followed—often included the hope that in the end, in the final judgment, this man would get what he actually deserved for murdering his wife. True justice demanded a punishment greater than the one delivered by the human court, and people counted on God to even the score. Although they didn't use the term, they depended on the future *wrath of God* to eventually deliver justice.

Deep down, we all know that if God is just, He can't let the really evil lawbreakers, like wife-murderers and rapists, escape the punishment they deserve. In cases like these, we cry out for the wrath of God, because we know for true justice to be done, God must do it.

But Scripture teaches that we are all offenders. We may not be murderers or rapists, but still, we all fall short of God's righteous requirements (Rom. 3:23). My little lie to my mother when I was five was an act of rebellion against the God who created me and ruled me. Yes, looking back, it seems like a small thing, but beneath my childhood sin was the same defiance of the holy God and His moral standards that lies beneath every human sin. Some sins are worse than others, and our just God will take this into account, but every time we break His rules for us, it's as if we are shaking our fists at Him, spitting in His face, and then trying to push Him off His throne. Every sin is an act of revolt against our rightful ruler.

We have all rebelled against God, so we all deserve His righteous wrath. None of us 'honor him as God' (Rom. 1:21), and in His righteousness He condemns us all.

POURED OUT IN HISTORY

God will express His wrath throughout eternity as He metes out just punishment for sin, but He has also expressed His wrath in history (Rom. 1:18). He has executed His judgment against sin using natural disasters, catastrophes, wars, and other tragedies. When God flooded the world in the time of Noah, He was expressing His wrath (Gen. 6:11–13). He poured out His wrath through the plagues in Egypt and the destruction of the Egyptian soldiers in the Red Sea (Exod. 7:3–5; Exod. 14:4, 17–18). Even the captivity of His chosen people was His judgment on them (2 Kings 17:1–23; 23:29–25:26). In New Testament times, God judged Ananias and Sapphira for lying to Him by immediately striking them dead (Acts 5:1–10).

We have no reason to think God's judgment through providential events stopped when the biblical record ended. Undoubtedly, He continues to mete out His wrath against sin right now as history unfolds. But since we don't have an inspired text to explain God's reasons for the calamities that have occurred since biblical times, we should be cautious in our conclusions about His specific purpose for any particular tragedy. Do you remember the man born blind that Jesus healed? The disciples assumed he was blind because God was judging him or his parents for their sin. But Jesus said otherwise. 'It was not that this man sinned, or his parents,' He told them, 'but that the works of God might be displayed in him' (John 9:1–3). This man's blindness was part of God's plan for Jesus to publicly heal him and bring glory to God, and not the result of God's judgment on him or his family. God has many purposes for human suffering, so not every tragedy is an expression of His judgment for sins committed by those who experience it.

God also pours out His wrath in history through the agency of human governments. When our governing authorities perform their judicial duties, they are instruments of God's justice, '[avengers] who [carry] out God's wrath on the wrongdoer' (Rom. 13:4). The judge's light sentence for the husband who murdered his wife in my home town is proof they don't always do their jobs perfectly, but still, God appoints our rulers to be agents of His wrath.

And God's wrath is expressed in history when He gives people up to act out their wicked passions (Rom. 1:24–31). Our merciful God is constantly working in the world to prevent people from acting on many of their destructive desires. When He withdraws His restraints and releases sinners to do the immoral deeds they want to do, He is carrying out His righteous judgment for sin. Moral degeneration in people and cultures, and the painful consequences that follow, are demonstrations of the wrath of God.

NO MORE FEAR

God's wrath is something all sinners—you, me, and everyone else—ought to fear. But it is also the backdrop for truly good news. Yes, the moment anyone sins they deserve God's wrath, but in His kindness, He delays His judgment to give people time to repent, receive forgiveness, and avoid His wrath altogether (Rom. 2:4).

And when God forgives, He does it in a way that is perfectly righteous. Christ's death provides the way for our righteous God, who can't simply overlook sin, to permanently turn His wrath away from sinners. As the apostle Paul explains in Romans 3:25–26,

> God put [Christ] forward as a propitiation by his blood … to show God's righteousness, because in his divine forbearance he had passed over former sins. It was to show his righteousness at the present time, so that he might be just and the justifier of the one who has faith in Jesus.

These may not be the easiest verses to understand, but they're two of the most important ones in the Bible. (This is neither the first nor the last time we look at them in this book.) We can paraphrase them like this. Christ's *propitiatory* (or wrath-appeasing) death proves to everyone that God is righteous, because even as He forgives sinners and permanently turns His wrath away from them, every sin receives the punishment it deserves. Jesus took upon Himself the sins of those who will be forgiven and bore the just wrath of God in their place. Through Jesus' death, God can forgive sinners in a way that is perfectly righteous. At the cross, He can justify sinners and still be completely just.

A few months after I lied to my mother and knew for the first time that I had offended God by my actions, I stood on the back pew of my small church and listened to the sermon. In it I heard an explanation of Christ's death on the cross, and in my mind I saw an image of Jesus on the cross, suffering for me. Right then I understood that I needed what was accomplished there. I heard the story of Christ's death and saw something wonderful: the beauty and wisdom of the cross. On this Sunday long ago, the holy God forgave my sin, and I no longer needed to fear His wrath.

Those of us who have been forgiven deserve to have God's wrath poured out on us, but we have been permanently spared instead, and all because of Christ's wrath-appeasing death. J. I. Packer writes:

> Between us sinners and the thunderclouds of divine wrath stands the cross of the Lord Jesus. If we are Christ's through faith, then we are justified through his cross, and the wrath will never touch us, neither here or hereafter. Jesus 'delivers us from the wrath to come.' (1 Thess. 1:10, RSV)[7]

As a matter of fact, it is because God is just that His wrath can never touch those who belong to Jesus. Once sins have received their deserved punishment in His death, it would be unjust for God to punish the sinner for those same sins, too. And God is never unjust.

Believers, then, should not fear the day of wrath. While we were once subject to God's wrath (Eph. 2:3), we have now been forever 'saved by [Jesus] from the wrath of God' (Rom. 5:9). Those of us who have experienced God's forgiveness will be grateful throughout eternity for Christ's wrath-bearing sacrifice.

God Tells It Like It Is: Truthfulness

> [T]he LORD is the true God; he is the living God and the everlasting King. (Jer. 10:10)

---

7   Packer, *Knowing God*, 156.

Do you trust the leaders who run your country? When they speak, do you assume they are telling the truth? Most of our earthly rulers aren't entirely truthful. In order to be elected, they promise to do things they don't really intend to do, and as soon as they come to power, they begin breaking those promises. Our leaders manipulate facts or deny them outright to make themselves and their policies look better than they are. No matter where you live, you can probably give examples of the untruthfulness of those who govern you. But there is no reason to doubt the truthfulness of our ultimate ruler, the God who created the universe and who governs it. He is 'the God of truth' (Isa. 65:16).

What does it mean for God to be truthful? *Truthfulness* is another of the attribute words that is difficult to define because both Scripture and books on theology use it to describe a few distinct but related aspects of His nature.

First, to say God is *true* means He is the one *real* God. As the true God, He is not created but rather, He created everything that exists. He is not like the false gods, who are nothing more than human creations. The false gods are made of dead wood, but the true God is the living God (Jer. 10:9–16). The true God has real power and does many praiseworthy works with His power. But false gods? They are powerless, worthless do-nothings (Ps. 96:3–6). The one true God—the *real* God—is everything God should be.

This doesn't mean He lives up to an outside standard of 'godness' to be the true God. Rather, in the same way that His own character determines the standard of true morality, His own character determines what a true God should be. He meets His own standard of true 'godness' by being Himself. What's more, He created us, His image bearers, with an innate sense of this standard. We know instinctively something of what a true

God should be, and we should be able to recognize Him as the one real God.[8]

Second, that God is *true* means He knows things as they really are. When we studied God's knowledge, we detailed all of the things He knows. That He is true means that everything He knows corresponds with reality. God's thoughts, then, are the final standard of truth. The proper goal for human learning, then, is to conform our thoughts to His thoughts. His thoughts are the foundation for any genuine human knowledge. It's only when we think what God thinks that we are thinking the truth.

Third, that God is *true* means every word He speaks is true (Prov. 30:5; Heb. 6:18; Titus 1:2). Since God's thoughts are the standard of truth, and what God says reveals His thoughts, His speech is also the ultimate standard of truth. Whenever we learn anything true, we are learning it from God's speech. When my grandchildren learn new truths about God in Sunday school, they are learning from what the true God has spoken about Himself in Scripture. Their teachers take the truths from God's word and teach them using language preschoolers can understand. And when they watch ducks dip in the pond, they learn how ducks eat—or rather, how God feeds ducks—from the truths He speaks into our world through His works of providence. Even when scientists learn something true, they learn it only because the true God has revealed it. When their experiments lead to new discoveries, they have simply used the thinking skills God gave them to discover the truths He has spoken through His creation of the world and His sustaining work in it.

Scripture, as God's direct speech and our clear window into His thoughts, is the standard by which we ought to judge the truthfulness of all human ideas and convictions. Philosophical arguments about what God must be can't override what His

---

8   Grudem, *Systematic Theology*, 195.

Word tells us about Him. The soundness of the arguments open theists make about God's knowledge of the future, for example, should be judged by what God says about Himself in the Bible. Some free-will theists argue that God doesn't know the future choices of human beings, because if He knew them, human beings would not have free will. From our human standpoint, this argument may seem to make sense; but when we judge it by what God says about Himself, we know it isn't right. In the Bible, the true God has told us that He is the one who declares the future (Isa. 46:9–10). According to Scripture, our ultimate standard of truth, God doesn't just know the future, but He determines it.

Everything God tells us about His creation in His Word is exactly right, too. If a scientific theory actually contradicts what He has told us in Scripture, then the scientific theory is wrong, not Scripture. Any theory not consistent with His Word can't be true because what God says is the standard of truth.

Did you know your own eternal life depends on the truthfulness of God's word? According to Jesus, 'This is eternal life,' that we know 'the only true God, and Jesus Christ whom [He has] sent' (John 17:3. The kind of knowledge Jesus speaks of is more than intellectual knowledge about God, of course, but it starts with intellectual knowledge. To have eternal life, we must first know about the true God and His Son, Jesus Christ, and we can only know about them because God has spoken. He has told us who He is and who Jesus is in Scripture. If He didn't speak truthfully, we would have no way to know God or Jesus Christ, and we couldn't have eternal life. But thankfully, God *is* true. We can trust what He says about Himself in the Bible, and as we read it, we can see and know Him as He is.

Those who know God should imitate His truthfulness. God's words represent things as they really are, and our words should square with reality, too. As people remade in His image, we shouldn't be flatterers, frauds or hypocrites. When we compliment others, our praise should be genuine. If we're selling something, we must represent the product honestly. When we speak about the details of our lives with others, we should be careful not to give false impressions that make us appear more talented, organized, or hard-working than we are. Being truthful doesn't require us to disclose everything to everyone—after all, God doesn't tell us everything, but only what He decides is right and good for us to know. There are many wise reason to choose not to share things we know and experience, but what we do decide to reveal should be sincere and true.

Finally, that God is *true* means He is *faithful*. He 'is not man, that he should lie,' so He always does what He says He will do (Num. 23:19; see also Titus 1:2 and Heb. 6:17–18). He will keep every one of His promises because He is true.

God's faithfulness is essential to the believer's assurance. Louis Berkhof explains:

> This faithfulness of God is of utmost practical significance to the people of God. It is the ground of their confidence, the foundation of their hope, and the cause of their rejoicing. It saves them from the despair to which their own unfaithfulness might easily lead, gives them courage to carry on in spite of their failures, and fills their hearts with joyful anticipations, even when they are deeply conscious of the fact that they have forfeited all the blessings of God.[9]

As the author of Hebrews said, God's faithfulness to keep His promises gives us 'strong encouragement to hold fast to the hope set before us' (Heb. 6:18). When we grow discouraged because of our lack of progress in holiness, our faithful God's promise to

---

9   Berkhof, *Systematic Theology*, 70.

save us anchors our souls (Heb. 6:19). When we grow frustrated with our inability to completely overcome sin, we can rest in our faithful God's promise that He will keep on working within us until His work is finished when Christ returns (Phil. 1:6). If you are a believer, you can be sure that because God is faithful, He will keep His promise to bless you eternally.

The faithfulness of God is another facet of His truthfulness that those who belong to Him should copy. We should be careful what we promise, but once we've promised, we should do everything we can to keep our word. Have you told your children you would do something special with them, or told a friend you would do a favor for her, and then avoided fulfilling your promise because you didn't really want to do what you said you would do? I have. But this is not the way our faithful God treats us, and it's not the way we should treat our children or our friends. Of course, we are not God, and sometimes circumstances we can't foresee keep us from doing what we say we will do. There will be times we can't fulfill our promises. Still, those who belong to Christ should be known for their faithfulness to keep their promises.

God's truthfulness is included here with His righteousness because His truthfulness has its source in His righteousness. God is faithful to His promises *because He is righteous* (Neh. 9:8). God is righteous, so He loves the truth, speaks the truth, and requires that we love the truth and speak the truth, too (Exod. 20:16).

Do you see God's glory in His holiness, righteousness, justice, and truthfulness? We know they contribute to His glory because, for one, when we aren't morally pure like God, when we don't live up to the standards set by His moral character, the Bible says we 'fall short of the *glory* of God' (Rom. 3:23, emphasis mine). Holiness, righteousness, justice, and truthfulness are aspects of the moral *perfection* of God. They are facets of His beauty. Even

God's wrath is glorious, not only because it is just and right for Him to condemn sin, but also because His wrath provides a foil for His love, grace, and mercy (Rom. 9:22–23). God's love, grace and mercy, which we take up in the chapter to follow, shine gloriously bright against the backdrop of His wrath.

Prayer

Holy God,

When I consider your holiness, I see how far I fall short of your righteous standards for me, and I know I deserve your condemnation. Thank you for making a way for me to have my sins forgiven and escape your righteous wrath.

Give me the desire and ability to follow your rules. Work within me to make me righteous like you are. Cause me to always speak the truth, keep me from making careless promises, and help me to joyfully keep the ones I make. Make me holy as you are holy.

QUESTIONS

HE IS HOLY

In His holiness, God is completely set apart from sin, so everything He does is perfectly righteous. He rules the universe in righteousness, giving us just and righteous laws to follow. But everyone breaks His laws, and as the perfect judge, He condemns us all. The good news is that Christ's death provides a way for our holy God to forgive us and still be perfectly just.

In His holiness, God is also true. Everything He knows and speaks is the truth. And because He is true, He is faithful to keep His promises to us.

1. Look up each of the texts below and identify the type of holiness described. Does it refer to God's *majesty-holiness* or His *ethical holiness*? Explain each of your answers.
   1. 1 Chronicles 16:27–30
   2. Isaiah 5:16
   3. Isaiah 57:15
   4. Acts 3:14
   5. Hebrews 7:26
   6. Revelation 4:8
   7. Revelation 6:10

2. Do you wish God's standards for human behavior weren't so high? Why can't we live up to His standards? How *should* we feel about His rules for us?

3. In Revelation 6:10, the souls of martyrs ask God to avenge their deaths by expressing His wrath against those who murdered them. Is it right for us, then, to ask God to bring justice for wrongs done against us? Explain your answer.

4. Why does understanding God's justice give believers confidence that they will never experience His wrath?

5. What can we know about Scripture because we know God is true? Explain your answer.

6. What is one way you fall short of God's standard of truthfulness? What are some steps you can take to better reflect His truthfulness?

7. Think of one reason to thank God for each of the attributes discussed in this chapter. Why are you thankful for His majesty-holiness? His ethical holiness? His justice? His truthfulness?

Chapter 6

He Is Good

One of my favorite autumn activities is picking the wild cranberries that grow on the mossy forest floor surrounding my home. Last fall they were so plentiful that I didn't need to harvest beyond the small strip of woods right across the street from my house. When the snow finally came, I had three large mixing bowls full of cranberries waiting to be turned into jam or juice, or frozen whole to use in muffins throughout the winter. Even so, I left plenty of berries on the bushes for the birds and bears.

Where I live in northern Canada, the wild bounty God provides includes cranberries (or lingonberries), caribou, moose, bison and more. In Minnesota where I grew up, He gives wild blueberries, chokecherries, juneberries, wild rice, and venison. From His goodness, God provides all of these native foods for His creatures to eat.

Even if you live where there isn't much wild food to hunt or gather, God provides the food you eat. Do you grow some of your own food? The vegetables and fruits you grow are His good gifts to you. If you buy your food in a local market or supermarket, God is using farmers, truckers, grocers, and others to supply food for you to eat.

No matter where we live, or how we gather it, we all receive our food from God's goodness. In this chapter, we will consider His goodness and three other related attributes. From God's goodness, love, mercy and grace, He gives us wonderful gifts— food, homes, families, and more. But even greater than these is His gift of His Son. From His goodness, God gave His own Son for our salvation.

God Gives : Goodness

The LORD is good to all … (Ps. 145:9)

The Father, Son, and Spirit exist in an eternal relationship of sharing and love,[1] and from the overflow of this eternal *goodness*, God gives good gifts to His creatures. The psalmist David described the *goodness* of God in Psalm 145:

---

1   Reeves, Michael, *Delighting in the Trinity: An Introduction to the Christian Faith* (Downers Grove, Illinois: IVP Academic 2012), 47.

> The LORD is good to all,
> and his mercy is over all that he has made.
> The eyes of all look to you,
> and you give them their food in due season.
> You open your hand;
> you satisfy the desire of every living thing. (Ps. 145:9, 15–16)

Our good God generously provides everything His creatures need.

The eighteenth-century English Baptist pastor John Gill described God's goodness as 'an inexhaustible fountain' overflowing forever even though He is continually sharing His goodness with the living things He has made.[2] In John Gill's time, city fountains didn't recirculate their water like the fountains we have now. Instead, they drew water from a reservoir or natural springs, and provided this clean water for all the people who lived around them. God's inexhaustible fountain of goodness is this kind of fountain—one that constantly provides us with fresh goodness. But with His fountain, there is no danger the reservoir will run dry or the springs will dry up. He has an eternal unlimited supply of fresh goodness. His goodness flows from Him forever in a never-ending stream.

From the abundance of His generosity, God grows mushrooms to feed squirrels and saplings to feed deer. He provides earthworms for robins and mice for foxes. The greens I grow in my garden come from His goodness, too. He could have created only one kind of salad green, or none at all, but instead, He created crispy romaine, buttery spinach, chewy kale, spicy arugula, and red leaf lettuce for extra visual punch, each variety increasing my pleasure as I eat my summer salads. Vegetables,

---

2   Gill, John, 'A Body of Doctrinal Divinity' Christian Classics Ethereal Library, http://www.ccel.org/ccel/gill/doctrinal.ii.xvi.html

fruits, grains, and meats, both wild and cultivated—every different kind is a good gift from our good God.

God directs everything in the universe, so every benefit we receive—every 'good gift'—comes from Him (James 1:17). Beyond our food, homes, and families, He gives us jobs, friends, vacations, sunshine, music, colors, and even the air we breathe. Everything that sustains us and everything that gives us joy— all are God's gifts to us. Even when people give gifts to us, underneath their gifts is the goodness of God. He gave them enough to share (1 Cor. 4:7) and the desire to share with us.

God is generous to everyone, even those who don't acknowledge Him or His gifts. '[H]e is kind to the ungrateful and evil,' Jesus said (Luke 6:35). '[H]e makes his sun rise on the evil and on the good, and sends rain on the just and on the unjust' (Matt. 5:44–45). Even God's enemies receive good gifts from Him.

This doesn't mean, however, that He distributes His gifts equally to everyone. As long as He gives no one less than they deserve, God can give more to some than others and still be perfectly just and good. He can do what He chooses with all that belongs to Him, and we have no right to complain or be envious of the gifts He gives to others (Matt. 20:13–15).

But we aren't always satisfied with what we receive from Him, are we? I sometimes envy retired couples who drive their motor homes through my town each summer. I was in my forties when my husband passed away, so I will never be able to take retirement road trips with him. Given the opportunity, we probably wouldn't have traveled much during our retirement years anyway, but knowing this doesn't keep me from coveting this gift God has given to others but not me. What gifts do you long for? A bigger and better house? A more challenging job? A more attentive husband? Whatever they are, when we envy the gifts God has given to others, we're rejecting His goodness, first, by begrudging His generosity to others, and second, by undervaluing the gifts He has generously given to us.

The first step to being satisfied with the gifts God has given us is to acknowledge them. We tend to take His generosity for granted because He is constantly providing for us from His abundance. We may commute to work, for instance, without considering that it is only because our good God is protecting us that we arrive safely. Or we may take a daily shower without acknowledging that God is the one who keeps the water pipes and the water heater working. But neither safe travels nor warm showers are automatic. They are both good gifts from God, gifts that some women won't receive today. When we remember His kindnesses to us—His big gifts and His small ones—and receive them with thanksgiving, we will be more content with what we have and less envious of His gifts to others.

From His goodness, God provides for the earthly needs of all His creatures, but for those who belong to Him, His generosity continues throughout eternity. Even in this life, every single circumstance is a good gift working an eternal purpose. All things, including life's trials, are part of God's benevolent plan to make every believer more like Christ (Rom. 8:28–29). Can you see why the apostle Paul reminds his readers to be thankful in all circumstances (1 Thess. 5:18)? Our generous God uses everything, even the hard things, to remake His people in His image.

He Provides For All!

And as those who are being remade in His image, God's people should reflect His goodness. Since He is good even to His enemies, we are called to be good to our enemies, too. And who are our enemies? When Jesus commanded His followers to love their enemies, He included a wide range of people in this category. According to Jesus, anyone who didn't love them, anyone who wasn't a brother to them, along with anyone who was actively persecuting them (Matt. 5:43–48), was an enemy. Every one of us has plenty of enemies to be generous to! The grumpy neighbor who doesn't like your family because she prefers silence to the sound of children playing in your backyard is, according to Jesus, your enemy. As His disciple, you are called to not retaliate, but to do good instead. If you take her a few fresh muffins, you are fulfilling His command to love your enemies. You are providing for someone who doesn't love you or your children, just as God provides for those who don't love Him or His children. Likewise, when you are kind to the co-worker who purposefully undermined you, you are imitating God's kindness to both the just and the unjust. And if you pray for someone who is hostile to you because of your Christian faith, you are also reflecting God's generosity to His enemies. You are following Jesus' command to be like 'your Father who is in heaven' (Matt. 5:45).

But just as God is especially generous to those who belong to Him, His people should be especially 'good to ... those who are of the household of faith' (Gal. 6:10). Yes, we should give to people in our neighborhoods and people across the world, but the priority for our generosity should be our fellow-believers. Even as we donate to needy children world-wide, our first duty is to make sure the needs of the children in our own churches are met.

And whenever we give to others—to our fellow believers, to the community around us, or to people far away—we are simply giving from what we have already received from God. Any praise we receive for our generosity should be redirected to Him, who gives to us so we can give to others. All the glory for both the gifts we receive and the gifts we give is rightfully His.

God Saves: Love

> For God so loved the world, that he gave his only Son ....
> (John 3:16)

Do you remember the woman who told me she didn't believe God would condemn anyone because the Bible teaches that He is love? She was wrong, of course, but not completely wrong. God *is* love (1 John 4:8). He is loving by nature, but His love doesn't eliminate all eternal condemnation. Rather, from His love God rescues some from condemnation.

Sometimes Scripture refers to God's general generosity to all His creatures and calls it *love*. For instance, when Jesus told His disciples to love their enemies because God loves His enemies by providing sunshine and rain for them (Matt. 5:44-45), He used the term *love* this way. But as a rule, when the Bible speaks of God's love, it refers to a specific aspect of His goodness— His *redemptive love*. His redemptive love is love that actually saves people.

The greatest demonstration of God's love was the gift of His Son for our salvation. 'In this the love of God was made manifest among us,' the apostle John wrote, 'that God sent his only Son into the world, so that we might live through him' (1 John 4:9). God showed us His love by sending 'his Son to be the propitiation for our sins' (1 John 4:10), even though we were God-haters in open rebellion against Him. Our loving God redeemed us 'while we were still sinners' and 'while we were [His] enemies' (Rom. 5:8, 10). There was no reason within us for God to love us, and worse, there was every reason for Him *not* to love us, but He still loved us and sacrificed His Son to save us. God's love is the kind of love that saves the unlovely, unworthy, and undeserving at great cost.

Nothing within the object of God's love draws His love from Him. Moses told the people of Israel that God loved them, 'not because [they] were more in number than any other people' —as a matter of fact, they were 'the fewest of all peoples'— but simply because He loved them. He had promised to love the offspring of Abraham, Isaac, and Jacob forever, and He was keeping His promise to these historical fathers when He loved their descendants (Deut. 7:7–8). In other words, God loved Israel, not because they attracted His love by their greatness, but because He decided to love them and because He promised their ancestors He would love them. God's love for them came from Himself—from His own choice and His own commitment. The cause of God's love for Israel was not in them, but in God.

The saving love God has for His new-covenant people follows this pattern, too. He saved us, Paul wrote, 'not because of our works but because of his own purpose and grace which he gave us in Christ Jesus before the ages began' (2 Tim. 1:9). His redeeming love flows to us because in eternity past He chose to save us and pledged to accomplish this saving purpose in history. He doesn't love us because of anything we are, or anything we do, but because He is love.

God's love isn't much like our natural human love, is it? We love because we are attracted by something in the one we love. A wife loves her husband because of certain qualities she sees in him. He may be dependable, or strong, or good-natured, or handsome, and so she loves him. Children naturally love their parents because their parents love, provide, and care for them. And why do parents love their children? Because children are born tugging at our heartstrings. We have a natural connection to our own offspring, and we can't help but love them. Our love is drawn from us by those we love. Even our love for God works this way. If we love Him, it is because we see His beauty and know what He has done for us.

But God's love works the other way around. He loves us, not because of who we are or what we've done, but because of who He is. This is the only way it can be for a God who exists from Himself. If something in us caused Him to love us, His love would be drawn from Him by factors outside Himself, and it wouldn't be independent—or 'from Himself'— love. As the great preacher Charles Spurgeon said in one of his sermons, 'The Lord loves you not to-day, Christian, because of anything you are doing, or being, or saying, or thinking, but He loves you still, because His great heart is full of love, and it runneth over to you.'[3]

God's redemptive love is love that actually saves people. Unlike His providential love, which generously provides for all His creatures, God's redemptive love is not universal. (If it were, everyone would be saved.) Rather, His redemptive love is a special love He has for His own people. It is the love with which 'Christ loved the church' and from which He 'gave himself up for her' (Eph. 5:25). From His redemptive love, God appointed people to be His adopted children (Eph. 1:5) and then redeemed them (Eph. 1:7). With His redemptive love, He gives His children new life (Eph. 2:4–5) and disciplines them to keep them faithful to Him (Heb. 12:5–8). This special love God has for His own is for all believers together, but also for each believer individually. If you believe, you can join with the apostle Paul when He says Christ 'loved *me* and gave himself for *me*' (Gal. 2:20).

God's love, like each of His attributes, is infinite. King David describes it as 'great *to* the heavens,' in one psalm and 'great *above* the heavens' in another (Ps. 57:10 and 108:4, emphasis mine).

[handwritten margin note: Do we miss this love to unbelievers? Reprosent Do we miss this love to unbelievers?]

---

3   From 'The Perfuming of the heart', accessed at http://www.biblia.work/ sermons/the-perfuming-of-the-heart/

'The measure of love,' J. I. Packer wrote, 'is how much it gives, and the measure of the love of God is the gift of His only Son to become human and to die for sins ....'[4] The Father sent His Son—the Son beside Him and equal to Him, the Son whom He loved and who returned His love eternally—to suffer for unworthy sinners who hated Him. No wonder the apostle Paul wrote that the measure of God's love 'surpasses knowledge.' Even so, as believers, we can know this infinite love of God as we are 'filled with all the fullness of God' (Eph. 3:18–19).

God's love is also eternal and unchanging. According to Jesus, the Father loved the Son 'before the foundation of the world' (John 17:24), so we know the persons of the Trinity exist eternally in a relationship of love. Their mutual love had no beginning and it will have no end, and from the abundance of His eternal Trinitarian love, God loves His children. If you are a believer, God loved you in eternity past 'before the foundation of the world' (Eph. 1:4–5) with His unchanging love (see Ps. 5:7, 6:4; 33:22 and many more). His love for you remains as strong forever as it was in eternity when He chose to love you, and when, in love, He sent His Son into history to die for you.

The apostle Paul wrote a long list of things that can't separate those who belong to God from His eternal love. 'Shall tribulation, or distress, or persecution, or famine, or nakedness, or danger, or sword?' he asks. The right answer is *no*! What about death or life, angels or rulers, things present or things to come? Or powers, heights, or depths? It's *no* to each of these, too. For good measure Paul adds one last item to his list: *anything else in creation* (Rom. 8:35–39). This locks it up tight. Absolutely nothing that exists can stop the flow of God's love to the believer.

---

4   Packer, J. I., *Knowing God* (Downers Grove, Illinois: InterVarsity Press 1993), 125.

If you are God's child, you can be certain He will continue to love you for all eternity with His unchanging love. Family or friends may reject you, but God will still love you. His love will continue to abide with you even as your children grow up and leave your home to make their own. You may lose your parents, your husband, or other loved ones, but God's love for you will last for all of this life and on throughout eternity. You are completely secure in God's love!

LOVING LIKE GOD LOVES

Jesus instructed His disciple to love like He loved. 'Just as I have loved you,' He said, 'you also are to love one another' (John 13:34). In fact, love for others is the hallmark of His true followers. 'By this all people will know that you are my disciples,' He continued, 'if you have love for one another' (John 13:35). Those who belong to Jesus love their Christian brothers and sisters (1 John 2:10; 3:10)—and they love them sacrificially. Like Him, they are willing to give their lives for their friends (John 15:12–13; 1 John 3:16).

But there's more to God-like love than loving fellow believers. Did you know that when God loved you—when He sent His Son to bring you to Himself—you were His enemy (Rom. 5:8, 10)? You were not just a little lukewarm toward Him, but actually hostile (Rom. 8:7; Col. 1:21). How can we be like God and love others like *this*?

We've already discussed doing good to our enemies, but loving them like God loved us asks even more from us. God-reflecting love demands self-sacrifice. It requires a willingness to put the well-being of our enemies ahead of our own.

Do you remember the early Christian martyr Stephen? As a mob stoned him to death, he didn't ask God to avenge his murder, but asked Him to not hold this sin against them (Acts

7:59–60). This is a biblical example of the kind of love for one's enemies that reflects God's redemptive love.

I can think of others examples of those who loved their enemies sacrificially, too. I was born the year before five missionaries, including Jim Elliot, were killed by warriors from the Huaorani tribe they were trying to reach with the gospel. These men understood the dangers of their mission, but they were willing to risk their own lives for people who turned out to be their enemies. And Jim Elliot's wife Elisabeth later returned with her young daughter to serve these same people. They were responsible for her husband's death, but she loved them and was willing to also pour out her life so they could know the gospel.

You and I may never be called to knowingly risk death for the sake of our enemies, but we will be called to give up other things we value, like money, or reputation, or comfort. God calls His own to sacrifice so those who are hostile to Him—and hostile to them as well—can hear the good news of His saving love.

If you have genuine love for others, both your friends and your enemies, it is evidence you have been born again by the Spirit of God (1 John 4:7). When we love like God loves, our love is not really our own, but comes from Him and is communicated to us by His Spirit who lives within us (1 John 4:12–13, 16; Gal. 5:22). Any praise we receive for the love we show to others rightly goes to God, who first loved us so we would love like He does (1 John 4:19).

God Helps: Mercy

… his mercy is over all that he has made. (Ps. 145:9)

This year my church began sponsoring a family of refugees from Syria. The Canadian government will provide half the income they need for their first year here in our city, but we are responsible for the other half. This family was, of course, eager to leave the constant threats of violence that marked their life in Syria for the safety of life in Canada, but they don't know English, they have no experience with winter, especially our extreme northern ones, and they left all of their extended family and friends behind. Can you imagine how difficult their new life is? How lonely they can feel? Easing their transition to life here is also the job of the people in my church, and they need our help with all these things and more. A few weeks after they settled into the home prepared for them, they visited our Sunday morning service to thank us for helping them. The mother of the family stood in front of the congregation and cried as she spoke. 'We are not of your religion,' she said through a translator, 'but you have shown us mercy.'

She was using the word *mercy* the same way the Bible does. When the authors of Scripture use this word, they were focusing on the helplessness of those receiving mercy. In His mercy, God is good to those who are in trouble and need to be rescued from it. From His mercy He helps the helpless and gives hope to the hopeless.

God's mercy includes His pity for those who are in trouble, but it's more than mere pity, because His mercy has all of His power behind it. A leper once came to Jesus, and asked to be healed. 'Moved with *pity*, [Jesus] stretched out his hand and touched him and said to him, "… be clean." And immediately the leprosy left him' (Mark 1:41–42, emphasis mine). Jesus saw this man's predicament, sympathized with him, and used His infinite power to cure him. This is how it works with God's mercy. From His mercy, He helps those no one else can help. God's mercy accomplishes what is impossible for anyone but Him.

In His mercy, God heals the sick, provides for the needy, and rescues those who are exploited and mistreated. From His mercy,

He delivers people from affliction, oppression, and poverty. He is '[f]ather of the fatherless and protector of widows' (Ps. 68:5; see also Ps. 10:14; Hosea 14:3) because He is merciful. Since everything God created is dependent on Him, everything He does to sustain His creatures is an act of mercy. The food we eat, the water we drink, the air we breathe, and everything else that keeps us alive—all are gifts from the mercy of God. Can you see why David's psalm says, 'his mercy is over all that he has made' (Ps. 145:9)?

But whenever God helps, it is always because of His independent decision to extend mercy. 'I will have mercy,' He said, 'on whom I have mercy' (Rom. 9:15). When He deals mercifully with anyone, it is because He is a God of mercy and has chosen to be merciful to them (Rom. 9:16, 18). He is never merciful because of the good works someone has done, but always 'according to His own mercy' (Titus 3:5; see also Rom. 9:16; Eph. 2:4–9).

At the same time, Scripture teaches that those who humbly ask God for mercy are sure to receive it. He isn't compelled to be merciful to us, and we certainly don't want to presume on His mercy, but as His children, we can be confident that when, in our weakness, we ask Him for help, He, in His mercy, will help us (Heb. 4:16; Ps. 86:5–7).

DEEPEST MERCY

God's ultimate act of mercy was sending His Son to die to deliver people from sin. If you are a believer, you were once helpless and hopeless, but in His mercy, God sent His Son to be your Savior (Luke 1:76–79). Could you have saved yourself? Freed yourself from slavery to sin? Could you have opened your own spiritually blind eyes? Raised yourself from spiritual death? No, you were completely dependent on God's help. In mercy

Christ died for you, in mercy God cleansed you from sin, and in mercy the Spirit empowers you to obey (Titus 3:3–5). You had no hope until your merciful God 'caused [you] to be born again to a living hope' (1 Pet. 1:3). You have been saved because God is 'rich in mercy' (Eph. 2:4–5). You belong to Him because you have received His mercy (1 Pet. 2:10).

There is no limit to the mercy of God. 'His mercies never come to an end,' but are 'new every morning' (Lam. 3:22–23). God's mercy is an inexhaustible fountain, too. Every day is a fresh opportunity to experience new mercies from His never-ending, never-run-dry supply. From God's infinite mercy, there is always more help for you.

And every day is a fresh opportunity for God's children to 'be merciful, even as [our] Father is merciful' (Luke 6:36). Indeed, one of the reasons God chose to be merciful to us is so we will be merciful to others. He 'comforts us in all our affliction, so that we may be able to comfort those who are in any affliction, with the comfort with which we ourselves are comforted by God' (2 Cor. 1:4). In His mercy, God saw our need and rescued us, and now He invites us to imitate Him by helping those who need our help.

When you care for your sick children—rocking them to sleep, giving them medicine, wiping their noses, or mopping up after they throw up—you are reflecting the mercy of God. If you help your elderly neighbor with yard work he's too frail to finish on his own, you are showing him mercy. When people from my church donated clothing, furniture, or money to support the Syrian family, they were instruments of God's mercy. And when we share the gospel, the story of God's mercy to sinners, we are giving hope to the hopeless like our merciful God gives hope to the hopeless. Any poverty, weakness, illness, pain, or hopelessness we see is an opportunity for us to show mercy because God has shown us mercy.

God Receives the Glory: Grace

> [A]ll have sinned and fall short of the glory of God, and are justified by his grace as a gift … (Rom. 3:23–24)

From His *grace* God is kind to those who only deserve His judgment for their sin. God's mercy and grace are both aspects of His goodness to us, but His mercy focuses on our helplessness, and His grace on our unworthiness.

Anything that comes from God's grace is a gift. It isn't, and it *can't* be, earned or merited. The apostle Paul wrote about God's choice of a remnant from the nation Israel and said if His choice 'is by *grace*, it is no longer *on the basis of works.*' In other words, if the people God chose had earned His choice, His choice wouldn't be a gracious one. If we could merit what comes from God's grace, His 'grace would no longer be grace' (Rom. 11:6). Paul's whole argument rests on the meaning of the word *grace.* Something received by grace is a gift, and anything earned is not a gift, but payment for work done. By definition, then, grace is incompatible with human merit. If our salvation is all of grace— and it is—we can't earn or merit any of it. And Paul confirms this elsewhere, too. Our salvation, he writes, is only 'by grace.' It is God's gift to us and not 'a result of [our] works' (Eph. 2:8–9; see also 2 Tim. 1:9; Rom. 3:20–24).

Theologians sometimes speak of *common grace.* When they use this term, they are referring to the gracious benefits God gives to all people from His general goodness or love for all humankind. From His common grace, God sustains life, restrains evil, and temporarily withholds His judgment for sin. He dispenses human talents and abilities—musical talents, physical or artistic abilities, intellectual or organizational skills, and more—and all of humanity profits from these gifts. Our governments are instruments of His common grace when they maintain order in society and promote prosperity. Since no one deserves anything but immediate judgment from God, any benefits we receive from Him are unmerited gifts from His grace.

But when Scripture speaks of God's grace, it is almost always referring to His *special grace,* the grace through which He actually saves sinners. Special grace isn't universal, but is given only to those God saves. In eternity past God graciously chose some to save (Eph. 1:3–6; 2 Tim. 1:9), and in time, He graciously calls (2 Tim. 1:9), regenerates (Eph. 2:4–7), justifies (Rom. 3:24; Titus 3:7), sanctifies (Titus 2:11–12), and preserves them (1 Pet. 1:3–5). From His grace, God sent His Son Jesus Christ to redeem those He chose to save, a redemption they receive through faith in Christ (Rom. 3:24–26). And even the faith in Christ through which they are saved is God's gracious gift to them (Acts 18:27; Eph. 2:8–9; Phil. 1:29).

Our salvation is entirely a work of God's grace. We contribute nothing. (Remember, if we did—if even the smallest piece of our salvation were based on our own work—'grace would no longer be grace.') As products of God's rescuing and recreating work, and not our own work, we will be everlasting demonstrations of 'the immeasurable riches of his grace' (Eph. 2:4–10). Our God is truly the 'God of all grace' (1 Pet. 5:10), because from start to finish, He saves His people by His grace.

God must save us by grace because we don't deserve to be saved. That our salvation is by grace alone presupposes our unworthiness to receive it. Are you a believer? What you deserve from God is judgment for your sin, but from His grace you are receiving the undeserved blessings of salvation instead.

And since it's only because of God's gracious work that anyone is saved, none of us can 'boast in the presence of God' (1 Cor. 1:29–30). We did nothing to save ourselves, so there is no room for human pride. Who deserves the glory for our salvation? Our gracious God who did all the work to save us. All glory goes to Him: 'Let the one who boasts,' Paul wrote, 'boast in the Lord' (1 Cor. 1:31).

Indeed, God's ultimate purpose for His whole plan of salvation is His own glory, especially the glory of His grace. He saves us by grace alone so we will know the richness of His grace (Eph. 2:7) and praise Him for it (Eph. 1:6). He saves us by grace so we will eventually stand together in eternity with all those who have been saved and praise Him for His glorious work of salvation. Think of it! 'A great multitude … from every nation, from all tribes and peoples and languages, [will stand] before the throne and before the Lamb, clothed in white robes, with palm branches in their hands, and [cry] out with a loud voice, "Salvation belongs to our God who sits on the throne, and to the Lamb!"' (Rev. 7:9–10). Everything will finally be as it should be because our good and gracious God will be receiving all the glory for all of eternity.

Prayer

Good and gracious God,

Thank you for all the gifts you have given me from the abundance of your goodness, for everything that sustains me from day to day, and everything that gives me joy. Most of all, thank you for your greatest gift, the gift of your Son to save me.

Create in me a love for others that reflects your love for me. Show me how to mirror your mercy by helping those who need my help. And may I trust your gracious work alone for my salvation, and give you all the glory for it.

QUESTIONS

HE IS GOOD

From His goodness, God provides for His creatures. Everything we have comes from Him. From His love, He sent His Son to redeem His people. In His mercy, He heals the sick, feeds the hungry, and delivers those who are oppressed. From His grace, He saves sinners who are unworthy of salvation and can do nothing to merit it. Salvation is accomplished through God's gracious work alone, so all the glory for it goes to Him.

1. Read Psalm 104. Make a list of things God provides for His creatures. Thank Him for each one.

2. Can you think of one gift God has given you today? How can you use it for His glory? Can you be generous to others with it?

3. If God were not triune, could His love be eternal? If He were not triune, could He be loving by nature? Explain your answers. 2 Cor 13:14

4. How is our natural human love different from God's love?

5. Think of an occasion when you needed help and God helped you. Have you thanked Him for His mercy to you?

6. Read Hebrews 4:16 and Luke 18:9–14. What do these verses teach us about the right way to approach God when we need His help?

7. Do you know someone who needs help? How could you help? How can you imitate your Father's mercy to you by showing mercy (Luke 6:36)?

8. Are you a believer? If so, you have received God's *special grace*, the grace that actually accomplishes salvation. What are some of the blessings you have received—and are receiving—from this special grace of God?

9. How can you be gracious to others like God has been gracious to you?

1. Provision of Food & Water, Shelter, Time, Work, God's Spirit

3. Inorder For there to be love God First had to love himself (The three).

4. Ours is attraction & conditional Pg.132

6. In humility w/ a pure intention heart, Confidence in Christ Approaching w/ Faith like a Child.

Chapter 7

He Planned and Created

Do you have a plan for tomorrow? Each night before I go to bed, I write a list of the next day's tasks, but more often than not, the next day doesn't go according to my plan. Something I didn't anticipate will happen and I'll need to make adjustments to my schedule. Yesterday I'd planned to spend the first half of the day working at my desk, but as I returned from my morning walk with the dog, my neighbor called me over and we ended up chatting for nearly an hour. Our unplanned conversation meant one less hour spent on the paper work I'd planned to complete, so I started today finishing up a job I'd originally scheduled for yesterday.

Some people keep to a schedule better than I do, but we are all only a stomach virus, plumbing disaster, chatty neighbor, or teething baby away from abandoning some of our plans for the day. Our firmly established plans are still provisional. 'Come now,' the apostle James wrote in his New Testament letter,

> you who say, 'Today or tomorrow we will go into such and such a town and spend a year there and trade and make a profit'— yet you do not know what tomorrow will bring. What is your life? For you are a mist that appears for a little time and then vanishes. Instead you ought to say, 'If the Lord wills, we will live and do this or that.' (James 4:13–15)

We can't even be sure we will make it to tomorrow, let alone carry out our plans. We can promise to do something, and even ink it in our day-planner, but there's always one caveat: *If the Lord wills*. We can only do what we plan to do as long as God wills for us to do it. Our plans are always dependent on God's plan. 'Many are the plans in the mind of a man,' the proverb says, 'but it is the purpose of the LORD that will stand' (Prov. 19:21). Our plans are never carved in stone, but God's plan always is. It is His plan that governs all other plans.

In the previous chapters, we studied God's nature, or what He is like in Himself. Now we're turning to His work in the universe. We begin our study with a discussion of God's comprehensive plan, something we also discussed when we studied His knowledge and wisdom. Since His plan is the blueprint for all of His work, we're returning to it briefly to lay the foundation for our study of what He has done, is doing, and will do in His creation.

God's Game Plan

> The counsel of the LORD stands forever,
> the plans of his heart to all generations. (Ps. 33:11)

God's unchanging plan for the course of history is officially called His *eternal decree*. The Westminster Confession of Faith describes His decree like this:

> God from all eternity, did, by the most wise and holy counsel of His own will, freely, and unchangeably ordain whatsoever comes to pass. . . .[1]

That God ordained something simply means He put it in His unchanging plan. According to the Westminster Confession, before God created anything, He decided everything that would happen from the moment of His first creative act on into the unending future. He ordained it all.

The men who wrote the Confession took this truth directly from Scripture. God's eternal plan is mentioned in Ephesians 1:11, which says God 'works all things according to the counsel of his will ....' Here the apostle Paul calls God's plan the *counsel of His will*.[2] God has a plan, Paul wrote, a plan which includes 'all things,' and He works everything out exactly as He has planned. When God created the universe, He was implementing His plan to create. As He governs His creation, He does as He ordained in eternity. And as He saves those He chose to save 'before the foundation of the world' (Eph. 1:4), He is 'working all things

---

1   Beeke, Joel R. and Sinclair B. Ferguson, eds., *Reformed Confessions Harmonized* (Grand Rapids, Michigan: Baker Books 1999), 29.

2   Other scriptural terms for God's decree or plan are *God's will* and *God's purpose*.

together for good ... to those who are called according to his purpose' (Rom. 8:28). All that has happened, is happening, and will happen was planned by God in eternity.

His plan encompassed everything—all the free acts of His creatures (Eph. 2:10; Gen. 50:20; Acts 2:23, 4:27–28), and every means by which His planned goals are achieved (2 Thess. 2:13).[3] Throughout history and into the never-ending future, God has worked and will work in every event and every circumstance to accomplish His decree.

That God will carry out His plan—that He will work 'all things according to the counsel of his will'—is so certain that Paul can speak of those who have been predestined to obtain an inheritance as having already obtained it (Eph. 1:11). Those God planned to save don't have their inheritance yet (Eph. 1:14), but we know they will inherit it for sure because God has included it in the counsel of His will. God decreed it, so it's as good as theirs already.

Since God brings everything to pass exactly as He planned, nothing that happens is meaningless. Every circumstance is planned by God for His own wise reasons, so every circumstance fulfills His purpose. When a stomach virus sends you to bed for the day, it will cancel your plans, but never God's plan. He is achieving His purpose for your life, and for creation, too, through things as ordinary as your minor illnesses. When my neighbor called me over for a chat, God was accomplishing His perfect plan for my life, for my neighbor's life, and for the history of the universe. I don't know God's purpose for our conversation, but I do know He has one. In His eternally decreed universe, no event or circumstance is pointless, although it may seem like it to us. He is always working in everything to accomplish His decree,

---

3   Berkhof, Louis, *Systematic Theology* (Grand Rapids, Michigan / Cambridge, U. K.: Wm. B. Eerdmans Publishing 1996), 105.

so everything in the history of the world and the story of our lives, including each small and seemingly insignificant detail, has meaning. Everything that happens is significant to God because everything that happens is a piece of His perfect plan to show His glory in the universe He created.

Out of Nothing by His Word

> [T]he universe was created by the word of God, so that what is seen was not made out of things that are visible. (Heb. 11:3)

The Bible begins with God's first act in the execution of His decree: 'In the beginning, God created the heavens and the earth' (Gen. 1:1). The first thing on God's eternal to-do list was to create the whole universe. Underneath His creative acts, supporting the existence of everything, was His will or plan. It is 'by [His] will they existed and were created' (Rev. 4:11). God created the world, not because of any need He had (Acts 17:25), but because He had a plan to accomplish.

You've probably heard the saying, 'You can't get something from nothing.' It's true, or at least it's true for us. We can't get something from nothing. But according to the Bible, God can! As He created, what had not existed began to exist (Rom. 4:17). Latin-loving theologians call His creative work *creation ex nihilo*, or creation 'out of nothing,' because there was nothing at all, and then from nothing He made the entire universe—all the stars, and all the planets, including our earth and everything in it.

I had a friend who knitted beautiful sweaters from wool yarn. She didn't buy the yarn she used, but she spun it herself. She started her creative work one step farther back in the creative process than most artists do because she made the medium used for her creations. Still, she didn't make the wool her yarn was spun from, but bought it from someone else. She began her projects with pre-existing raw material. But when God created the universe, He didn't use pre-existing material. There wasn't any. His act of creation was the beginning of everything, including the raw material of creation. He didn't create by simply shaping and ordering what was already there, but He made the very 'stuff' of the universe out of nothing. Even time itself began when God created it. '[C]reation and history,' writes Michael Horton, 'came into being together through God's *ex nihilo* speech.'[4]

Along with the material world, God created the spiritual one. He created the spiritual powers, the invisible 'thrones or dominions or rulers or authorities,' including all the angels (Col. 1:16; Neh. 9:6). No spiritual power (except God Himself) is eternal, but God created them all from nothing.

And God created all these things by *word* power. He simply spoke 'and it was so' (Gen. 1:3, 6–7, 9, 11–12, 14–15, 20, 24, 26). 'By the word of the LORD the heavens were made,' the psalmist wrote, 'and by the breath of his mouth all their host. For he spoke, and it came to be; he commanded, and it stood firm' (Ps. 33:6, 9). God said, 'Let there be ....'—and there were. No wonder the Bible speaks of 'the word of his power' (Heb. 1:3)! Theologians have a Latin term for this aspect of creation, too. He created by *fiat*—or by command. God commanded the world to come into existence, and at His command, the world came.

If you have trouble wrapping your mind around these truths, you're not alone. 'To say that [God] created 'out of nothing,' J. I. Packer writes, 'is to confess the mystery, not explain it.'[5] How could we explain it? Only God has the ability to speak things into existence from nothing (Rom. 4:17). Only He has words that

---

4   Horton, Michael, *The Christian Faith: A Systematic Theology for Pilgrims on the Way* (Grand Rapids, Michigan: Zondervan 2011), 326.

5   Packer, J. I., *Concise Theology: A Guide to Historic Christian Beliefs* (Carol Stream, Illinois: Tyndale House Publishers, Inc. 1993), 21.

give life where there was no life (John 5:25, 28). As creatures made in His image, we can create, but it's never *ex nihilo* creation. A potter creates from pre-existing clay. A woodworker creates with pre-existing wood and glue. My knitting friend started her creations with already existing wool from already existing sheep. We can rearrange and reshape already existing matter, but we can't make something from nothing. And we certainly can't speak anything into existence. But God can and He did. He commanded and everything came to be—the heavens and all the heavenly bodies, and the earth with all its plants and creatures (Ps. 148:1–12).

IT'S ALL GOOD

The story of God's work of creation is found in the first two chapters of Genesis. 'The earth was without form and void'— and it was dark (Gen. 1:2). The 'stuff' of the earth was there, already created by God, but the project was incomplete. He planned to continue His work by first shaping and arranging the world, and then by filling it with the plants and living creatures He had designed.

So God said, 'Let there be light,' and the light appeared (Gen. 1:3). It wasn't sunlight or moonlight—the sun and moon hadn't been created yet—but it was light provided by God. It was *good* light (Gen. 1:4), because it fulfilled His purpose. It did what He planned for it to do. Next God separated the light from darkness and gave them each a name—*day* for the light and *night* for the darkness. Then He established their order. After the darkness will come the light for the rest of the days of creation, and for all of the days of time. For the first three creation days, the pattern would be the same: God called things into existence, He gave them boundaries, and He named them. The story of the first day of creation ends with a refrain that is repeated after each of God's work days: 'And there was evening and there was morning, the first day' (Gen. 1:5).

God spoke again on the second day (Gen. 1:6–8) and called out an expanse to separate the water. He put some water above the expanse and some below, and then He named the expanse *sky*. Once more God created, divided, and defined—and then brought the evening and the morning to end day two.

On day three (Gen. 1:9–13), He gathered the water together to divide it from the land. He named the dry land *earth* and the collected water *seas*. With this, the ordering and arranging phase of creation was finished, and God began to fill the earth. From the land He called out plants and trees of many different kinds: fruit trees, pine trees, berry bushes, prairie grasses, wildflowers, and more. He created them ready to reproduce and fill the earth. On this day God prepared the earth for days five and six when He would call out the creatures who needed plants for food. Everything—earth, seas, plants, and trees—was *good*. Everything fulfilled its God-given purpose perfectly.

THE LIGHTS ARE WORKING

On the fourth day of creation (Gen. 1:14–19), God began to fill the space surrounding the earth. He said, 'Let there be lights in the expanse of the heavens to separate the day from the night' (Gen. 1: 14), and in response the sun, moon, and stars appeared, ready to serve His purposes. He had already given light and separated day from night on the first day; now He created heavenly lights to take over this job. Lighting the earth and separating day from night was their first purpose, but He gave them other purposes, too. '[L]et them be for signs,' God said, 'and for seasons, and for days and years' (Gen. 1:14).

Have you used the position of the sun to get your bearings while hiking, or to estimate the time of day? Have you seen the

Milky Way in the night sky and marvelled at the greatness of the God who made all the stars in our galaxy (Ps. 19:1)? If so, you've used the sun and stars as signs. They told you where you were, they showed you what time it was, and they pointed you to their Creator. And as they did, they were serving Him by doing what He meant for them to do.

God created the lights of the heavens 'for seasons, and for days and years,' too. He determined the length of our days, seasons and years when He planned and created the heavenly bodies, placed them in space, and began to move them in their courses.

Summer, fall, winter, and spring—all the earth's seasons are determined by the directness of the light from the sun. When the daily path of the sun is highest in the sky in my hemisphere, it is summer where I live. Unless it's raining, I have my morning coffee on the front porch to catch the warm breeze. When the sun's path is closest to the horizon, the mornings are dark and cold, so I drink my coffee inside. As the directness of the sunlight changes, the seasons unfold, and the sun fulfills one more of God's purposes for it.

The length of the earth's days is defined by the cycling sun— or more precisely, by the rotating earth, which looks like the cycling of the sun to us. One rotation of the earth—sunrise to sunset to sunrise again—marks the twenty-four hours of a day. As sunrise follows sunrise, over and over, the earth and the sun are marking the days as God intended for them to do.

God also made the lights in the sky 'for years.' The length of our year is established by the movement of the earth around the sun. From the beginning, people could measure each year—one revolution of the earth around the sun—by the placement of the sun and stars in the sky. As the lights in the sky mark the years, they are serving God by fulfilling a purpose He gave them.

As the fourth day ended, God saw that His new lights were good. They served their Maker and His purposes as they separated day and night, acted as signs in the heavens, and determined the seasons, days, and years.

ALL GOD'S CREATURES HAVE A PLACE

On day five (Gen. 1:20–23), God called out creatures to fill the sky and the seas, and in response, flying birds, schooling fish, breaching whales, and diving dolphins appeared. As He created, God defined all His creatures and gave them their boundaries. He made each one 'according to its kind,' and gave each kind a place to live. On this day, God not only called His creative work *good*, but He also blessed His creatures: 'Be fruitful and multiply,' He instructed, 'and fill the waters in the seas, and let birds multiply on the earth.' As the creatures God made complied with His call to reproduce within their kind to fill the oceans, rivers, lakes, and sky, they thrived.

On God's final work day, the sixth (Gen. 1:24–31), He commanded the earth to 'bring forth living creatures according to their kinds.' And with these words, all the dry land creatures came to be— 'livestock,' like flocking sheep and plodding cattle; 'creeping things,' like scurrying rodents and slinking lizards; and 'beasts of the earth,' like padding lions and lumbering bears. Once again, God declared His creatures *good*. He was satisfied with this day's work—*so far*.

But His workday wasn't done. He planned to create one more kind of creature—human beings. So He 'created man in his own image, in the image of God he created him; male and female he created them' (Gen. 1:27). He distinguished humankind from all His other creatures by creating them separately, and creating them, both the man and the woman, in His likeness.

The first two human beings were the high point of God's creative work (Ps. 8:5–8), and they had special significance to Him. They were the one kind of living thing specifically made in His image. He shared some of His attributes with them, and these shared attributes gave them the ability to relate to Him. The man and woman were the only creatures who could understand God when He spoke, and the only ones who could speak back to Him.[6]

And now, just as God had blessed the sky and sea creatures on the fifth day, God blessed His human creatures. 'Be fruitful and multiply,' He commanded, 'and fill the earth ....' (Gen. 1:28). He commissioned them—and along with them all subsequent generations of humankind—to govern the earth wisely as His representatives and to use the resources He created for their benefit. We call God's instructions to the first couple the *creation mandate*.[7]

When God finished the sixth day's work—when all the creatures were made and all His instructions given—He surveyed the things He had made and was pleased with His work. His creative work was completed and everything in creation fulfilled its God-given purpose perfectly. He made the world by calling it into being, and now it 'answer[ed] back in a symphony of praise, each species chirping, barking, bellowing, or otherwise communicating its delight and dependence on God and each other.'[8] The whole created order reflected the beauty of the one who made it. The heavens and earth, and everything in them, declared the glory of God (Ps. 19:1). No wonder the creation story pauses at the end of the last day to emphasize God's delight

---

6   Carson, D. A., *The God Who Is There: Finding Your Place in God's Story* (Grand Rapids, Michigan: Baker Books 2010), 22.

7   Or as some call it, the *cultural mandate*.

8   Horton, Michael, *The Christian Faith*, 334.

in His handiwork: 'God saw everything that he had made, and *behold*, it was *very* good' (Gen. 1:31, emphasis mine).

Seventh-Day Beauty Rest

[O]n the seventh day he rested and was refreshed. (Exod. 31:17)

Then on the seventh day, God rested (Gen. 2:1–3). It's not that He stopped working altogether. The universe He created on days one to six didn't run on its own. No, it continued to exist and function on day seven only because He continued, second by second, to sustain it (Heb. 1:3; Col. 1:17). But now, even as He kept holding the universe together, God rested from His creative work. Louis Berkhof compared His seventh day rest to 'the rest of an artist, after he has completed his masterpiece, and now gazes upon it with profound admiration and delight, and finds perfect satisfaction in the contemplation of his production.'[9] God didn't rest because He was tired—He never grows tired (Isa. 40:28)—but He rested to focus on the beauty of His finished work.

And as He rested, He was also establishing a pattern of work time and rest time for the people He created. Later, this work/rest arrangement was received by Moses as part of God's law for the people of Israel. 'Six days you shall labor, and do all your work,' the fourth commandment said, 'but the seventh day is a Sabbath to the Lord your God' (Exod. 20:9–10). God gave His people six days to work, and then one to rest and focus on the beauty of the One who made them. When they kept the commandment to rest on the Sabbath, they were honouring their creator and shaping their lives around the example He set when 'in six days [He] made heaven and earth, the sea, and all that is in them, and rested on the seventh day' (Exod. 20:11).

---

9   Berkhof, Louis, *Systematic Theology*, 157.

Let Us Make

> [T]here is one God, the Father, from whom are all things ...
> and one Lord, Jesus Christ, through whom are all things ....
> (1 Cor. 8:6)

The creation account in Genesis leaves room for only one God, the God who created everything. What we can't know from Genesis is that this one Creator God exists as Father, Son, and Spirit, and all three persons participated in the creation of the world. Looking at the text from our vantage point after the revelation of the Trinity, we see two phrases that hint at collaboration in creation. First, when the earth was still empty and unformed, before God said, 'Let there be light,' the Spirit of God was there, 'hovering over the face of the waters' (Gen. 1:2). We know now that He was there waiting to begin His creative work. Second, on the sixth day of creation, God said, 'Let *us* make man in *our* image, after *our* likeness' (Gen. 1:26), indicating the one Creator God was also in some sense 'us.' These teasers would have been just enough to make a careful reader of Genesis wonder: *What was the Spirit of God? Why was it 'hovering over the face of the waters'? How is the one God 'us'? Why does He refer to His image as 'our' image?*

Scripture's later revelation of God's work in creation goes beyond mysterious hints and teaches more directly about the roles of the three persons of the Trinity. In 1 Corinthians 8:6, for instance, Paul wrote that all things exist *from* the Father and *through* the Lord Jesus Christ. And He writes again, in Colossians 1:16:

> For by [the Son] all things were created, in heaven and on earth, visible and invisible, whether thrones or dominions or rulers or authorities—all things were created through him and for him.

The Father initiated the work of creation; everything came from Him. But at the same time, everything was created *by* or *through* the Son (See also John 1:3; Heb. 1:2). The Son was the Father's agent—or to use a phrase from Michael Reeves, He was the Father's 'executive arm'[10]— in the creation of the universe.

Scripture says much less about the role of the Spirit in creation, but we do know He was there working. 'The Spirit of God has made me,' Elihu, Job's friend, said, 'and the breath of the Almighty gives me life' (Job 33:4; see also Gen. 2:7). According to Elihu, one of the roles of the Spirit, whom He also called God's 'breath,' is to give life to human beings. Doesn't this suggest that one of His roles in creation was to breathe life into the first man and woman? Later, in God's work of salvation, the Spirit will breathe spiritual life into people who are spiritually dead, a role that suits perfectly the one who breathed physical life into God's first human creatures.

And as God's 'wind,' the Spirit is also the one by whom 'the heavens were made fair' (Job 26:13). Does this mysterious poetic language mean the Spirit was the one who decorated our sky with a brilliant sun, a glowing moon, and millions of sparkling stars? Was He the artist who made the whole creation beautiful?[11]

Like the Son, the Spirit was the Father's agent in creation. All three persons of the Trinity—Father, Son, and Spirit—worked together to create the universe. We don't know exactly how this cooperation worked, but we do know creation is *from* the Father, *through* the Son, and *in* the Spirit.[12]

---

10   Reeves, Michael, *Delighting in the Trinity: An Introduction to the Christian Faith* (Downers Grove, Illinois: IVP Academic 2012), 50.

11   Reeves, Michael, *Delighting in the Trinity*, 51-52.

12   Berkhof, Louis, *Systematic Theology*, 129. Berkhof uses the words *out of* instead of *from* in regards to the Father.

Knowing Your Place

> The God who made the world and everything in it, being Lord of heaven and earth, does not live in temples made by man, nor is he served by human hands, as though he needed anything, since he himself gives to all mankind life and breath and everything. (Acts 17:24–25)

The biblical story of creation laid the groundwork for the rest of the story of the universe. It established and revealed the true relationships between God, His creatures, and the material world.

First, the creation account teaches us who God is in relation to His creation. If God existed eternally and then created everything out of nothing, He isn't part of His creation, and creation isn't part of Him. He is greater than the universe He made, and distinct from it (Ps. 113:4–6). What's more, since God existed as all that He is in eternity, we know He doesn't need His creation. He is completely independent of it. Creation, on the other hand, is entirely dependent on Him. The whole universe exists right now only because God made it and continues to sustain it. When we put these truths together, it's clear His existence is a whole different kind of existence than that of the things He has made. He is eternal, but the heavens and earth exist in time. He is infinite, but the universe He made is finite. He is separate from His creation and beyond it, or to use the proper theological term, He is *transcendent*.

Still, even as He transcends His creation, He is always involved in it. He may be 'high and lifted up ... inhabiting eternity,' but He is also 'with him who is of a contrite and lowly spirit' (Isa. 57:15). Or to put it another way, He is transcendent, but also *immanent*. Yes, He is the infinite Creator who can't be contained in the temples people make, but He is also 'not far from each one of us' (Acts 17:24, 27). When you feel alone in the world, God is present with you and active in your life. When you feel overwhelmed by your responsibilities, He is there helping you fulfill them. He exists everywhere in His creation, and He is constantly upholding everything and everyone, including you.

And as the creator of the universe, God owns and rules it all. He defines the things He made, He sets their limits, and He assigns their duties. Creatures don't define themselves, but are what God their creator, owner, and ruler says they are. He determines their place and purpose in His creation.

Our true place as human creatures is under God's rule. Our true purpose is to worship Him and do what He commands. Understanding and accepting our place and our purpose keeps us from thinking too highly of ourselves. It keeps us from setting ourselves up as our own rulers or gods, and it makes us willing servants of the God who made us.

But as human creatures we shouldn't think too little of ourselves, either. The creation story teaches us that we are not merely the final and most advanced of the living things God created, but His own image bearers and representatives. We were created with special significance. Every human life is valuable to Him. And like Adam and Eve, the first humans, we were created for a special purpose: to fill the earth, govern it wisely, and worship and love our Creator.

That we were created to be God's representatives on earth and given specific instructions in the creation mandate gives meaning to our relationship with our environment, with the animals, and with other people. It also gives meaning to the work we do. Since the fall of humankind, we can't fulfill God's mandate to us perfectly, but still, as we labor, we represent Him by filling and governing His creation.

Do you make things? As you create, you are imaging God by imitating His own creative work. Do you care for people or animals? When you do, you represent God as you protect and provide for His creatures. As you work, God cares for His creatures through you. Do you take care of children? Or do you teach them? When you do, you are nurturing the next generation of image bearers and carrying out God's instructions to fill the earth. Do you work for your government? You are God's representative as you work to maintain order in creation and support the prosperity of His creatures. Do you grow food or flowers? When you till the soil, plant seeds, water plants, and pull weeds, you are governing creation by using its resources to produce food to eat and flowers to enjoy. All work, unless it's immoral, fulfills the creation mandate in some way; so all work, even the most menial labor, has value and significance to God.

The biblical creation story also teaches us something about our proper relationship to the physical world. God called everything He made good, so we know physical things, our bodies included, are good gifts from Him. He created the material world for us to enjoy with thanksgiving. We can, of course, use material objects in ways that are immoral, but in and of themselves, they are good. However, if we love material blessings—our possessions, the natural world around us, or our own bodies—more than we love God, we are keeping them from fulfilling their purpose, which is to point us back to the One who gave them to us. We are free, and even encouraged, to delight in material things, but we must set our hopes on God, 'who richly provides us with everything to enjoy' (1 Tim. 6:17).

All of creation has one ultimate purpose: to reveal the glory of its Creator. As God's handiwork, the universe fulfills its purpose as it proclaims His glory (Ps. 19:1). As His human creatures, we fulfill our purpose by acting as His representatives in His creation. Others see God's glory as we image Him to them. And as believers become more like God through the power of His Spirit, we also become more able to reflect His glory to those around us.

What's more, when we thank our Creator for the good gifts we receive from the world He made, we are proclaiming His glory. And when see beauty in our world and look beyond it to the beauty of the One who made it, God is glorified. When we look through the lens of creation to see the glory of God, we are helping creation fulfill the purpose for which it was created, and we are fulfilling the purpose for which we were created, too.

Prayer

God of creation,

Thank you for creating the universe and everything in it. Thank you for the good gifts it provides for me. Thank you that I can see your glory as I enjoy its beauty. Give me delight in my material blessings, but keep me from loving them more than I love you.

Thank you for giving humankind, including me, special significance and value by creating us in your image. May I grow in my likeness to you so I can better govern and care for your creation as your representative. Remind me that even when my tasks are menial and repetitive, as I work, I am reflecting you and fulfilling your purpose for me.

QUESTIONS

HE PLANNED AND CREATED

God has an eternal decree—an unchanging, all-encompassing plan for history, and He is always working in everything to accomplish it. He began to implement His plan when He created the universe and everything in it—light, sky, seas, land, vegetation, sun, moon, stars, birds, fish, and animals. The high point of His creation is humankind, made in His own image.

As the Creator of the universe, God rules everything. He defines the things He created and He gives them purposes to fulfill. His ultimate purpose for His creation is to reveal His glory.

1. Read Acts 18:21, Romans 1:10, 15:32, 1 Corinthians 4:19, and 16:7–8. In each of these texts, Paul plans for his future. How certain is he that he will be able to carry out his plans? What could keep Paul from doing what he planned to do?

2. Do you plan for your future? Do you make a daily or weekly schedule? What are some similarities between your schedule or plan and God's eternal plan? What are some differences?

3. In Romans 11, Paul discusses God's plan for history. When he finishes his explanation of it, he responds in verses 33–36. Read his response. When you think about God's eternal plan, what is your response?

4. How does the natural world reveal the God who created it? Which of His attributes do you see revealed in it? (See Romans 1:19–20 for hints.)

5. What does the truth that God created *ex nihilo* tell us about Him? What does it tell us about matter, the 'stuff' of creation?

6. In the biblical creation story, God spoke things into existence. Can you think of any other instances in which God accomplished His plan by the power of His spoken word?

7. How is the sun used as a sign in Matthew 16:2–3? Are there other ways besides those listed in this chapter to use the sun or moon as signs?

8. Why did God create people? What were His purposes for them? Can you support your answers from Scripture?

9. How does the work you do fulfill the cultural mandate? How do you image God through your labor?

10. Do you do creative work? How is your creative work like God's creative work? How is it different?

11. Why are people accountable to God? *He is who we answer to. We are the created*

12. Is there any material thing you are tempted to love more than God? How can you ensure that it serves its God-intended purpose in your life?

Cultural Mandate
• So much of our daily lives are influenced by culture.

Chapter 8

He Upholds the Universe

Years ago, my husband and I came to a fuller understanding
of the *providence* of God. We began to see that God is always
working in everything to bring His perfect plan to pass, and that
He has reasons for everything He does, reasons we may not—
and often won't— understand. We became convinced that even

suffering and death, when they come, are God's chosen means to accomplish His wise purposes.

And then my husband became sick. It was cancer, already advanced and progressing so rapidly that the first prognosis was that he had only a few weeks, or perhaps only a few days, to live. In less than a week, he went from feeling strong enough to spend a day golfing with his friends to feeling too weak to leave his hospital bed.

Our circumstances changed so quickly that we had little time to reflect on our situation. I spent as much time as I could with him at the hospital, but I also had children who needed my attention. And when he had enough energy to think, he needed to concentrate on setting his affairs in order. But one of my first thoughts after we received the bad news was, '*This* is why God has been teaching us about His providence. He was preparing us for this trial.' From the start, knowing our suffering had come to us through the hands of our good God comforted us.

Soon we began to wrestle with hard questions. How would I continue to raise the two children who were still at home on my own? My husband's father had died when he was just a boy, and he felt this loss every day, so he wondered how he could prevent his own young son from growing up with the same hole in his heart. Our questions had no easy answers.

Still, our new understanding of providence continued to give us hope. We knew God allowed trials in the lives of His people as a way to accomplish His purposes. We had a theological framework with a place for suffering in the lives of God's people, so we didn't feel abandoned or betrayed by Him because He hadn't prevented my husband's illness. We continued to trust Him in the midst of our trial, and didn't have the crisis of faith we had seen others endure.

[Handwritten margin note: I feel like I can relate to that statement! (in our life style!)]

One couple we knew lost all faith in God when tragedy struck their family. They couldn't bring themselves to worship a God who would allow their son to die. Over time, they stopped believing God existed at all. Others we knew adopted unorthodox views of God as they wrestled with His role in their own family tragedies. After her child was injured, one of my friends came to believe that God has a general hands-off policy in the unfolding events of the world. Another acquaintance couldn't accept that God would foresee his particular tragedy and not prevent it, so he adjusted his view of God. He came to believe that God doesn't actually know what's going to happen.

This is why I love the doctrine of God's providence. I know from experience that an understanding of providence prepares a believer for the trials that will eventually come to all of us. I want every Christian to know that God is working in everything, including the hard things, for their good (Rom. 8:28), because knowing this will give them true hope in difficult circumstances. No one should have to wrestle with the question of God's relationship to human suffering while they're in the midst of it.

Leaving Nothing to Chance

[God] works all things according to the counsel of his will ....
(Eph. 1:11)

Providence is the term theologians use to refer to God's constant care for the universe He created. The word *providence* isn't found in Scripture, but the concept certainly is. Scripture teaches that God is always working in His creation, and He is constantly carrying out His plan in it. He doesn't relate to His creation like a clock-maker relates to a clock He has made. God didn't create the universe, wind it up, and then leave it to run on its own. No, when it comes to His creation, He is always hands-on. He runs the universe and orchestrates its history to accomplish His purposes.

We've already seen that God had a plan for the universe, and the first step in bringing His plan to pass was to create everything in the universe. All that He does after creation to accomplish His plan is His providence. His mighty acts recorded in the historical books of the Bible are works of providence. The promises and prophesies found in the Bible either came to pass or will come to pass through His providential acts.

But there's more to providence than what's specifically recorded, promised, or prophesied in Scripture. Providence is simply God working according to His plan. Since all of history was directed by God according to His plan, all of history was a work of His providence. The future, as it unfolds, will be His providential work, too. He will accomplish everything yet to come according to His plan. Every detail of every circumstance and every event—past, present, and future—is or will be an act of providence.

One common misconception about providence is that God works in all the big events of history, but the so-called inconsequential events take place outside of His providential control. But Scripture tells us God's plan for the world includes all the small details, like what happens on every single day for every single person (Ps. 139:16). As He carries out His plan, He controls many things that may seem unimportant. The exact number of hairs on my head, for example, seems insignificant to me. I wouldn't want to lose *all* my hair, but I could lose a few strands and not even notice. Yet in His providence, God determines exactly how many strands of hair I have (Matt. 10:30). He leaves nothing to chance, but controls everything, even the apparently inconsequential details.

Who Holds the Stars? (Preservation)

[I]n [Christ] all things hold together. (Col. 1:17)

One aspect of God's providence is His *preservation* of everything He made. Right now as you read, the universe exists only because God is sustaining it 'by the word of his power' (Heb. 1:3). He holds everything together and keeps it all working. Even the laws of nature don't run on their own, but keep functioning only as God preserves them. He holds the stars in the sky and the water in the oceans (Neh. 9:6). He makes the sun rise and sends the rain (Matt. 5:45). The fields grow grain and the trees bear fruit because God causes them to produce (Lev. 26:4; Deut. 11:14). In the creation story, we learned that producing seeds and fruit according to their kind is what God created plants to do (Gen. 1:11–12), but they can fulfill this purpose only because He preserves their fruit-bearing properties. Underneath the natural processes producing fruit on my backyard Saskatoon berry tree is God's hand hanging berries and His warm breath ripening them.

God's creatures live only because He keeps them breathing (Ps. 104:29). As long as His power preserves a sparrow, it continues to exist (Matt. 10:29). I am alive at this moment because God is still giving me 'life and breath and everything' (Acts 17:25). When He withdraws His life-sustaining power, I will die (Job 34:14–15). And it's the same for everyone. We live because God gives us life, and we die because He takes our life away (Job 1:21).

Before God created, nothing else and no one else existed. Without His upholding power, everything and everyone but God Himself would no longer exist. As Louis Berkhof explained, 'it would not require a positive act of omnipotence on the part of God to annihilate created existences. A simple withdrawal of support would naturally result in destruction.'[1] If God stopped preserving His creation—poof!—it would disappear. Creation's continued existence is entirely dependent on His constant preservation.

Who Feeds the Ravens? (Concurrence)

Who provides for the raven its prey ...? (Job 38:41)

The area I live in is known for its large population of ravens. Like many others who live here, I have a love-hate relationship with them. Ravens are scavengers, and if I don't lock the lid tight on my garbage bin during winter, they will steal my food waste and spread the leftover packaging in the street. I once saw a raven fly off with a chunk of cheddar cheese snatched from a bag of groceries left in the back of a pickup in a supermarket parking lot. I've also seen one flying with an entire road-killed squirrel in its beak. As you can see, ravens aren't picky. They eat what they find—dead animals, live prey, duck eggs, wild berries, unguarded groceries, or garbage.

Their propensity to steal garbage and food is certainly annoying, but still, it's hard not to admire their intelligence. Ravens are the greedy geniuses of the bird world. They cache food for later, and they can find it when they need it because they remember where they put it. Ravens sometimes spy on other ravens to see where they stash their scavenged goodies, and then return when the coast is clear to steal their neighbor's food. And a hoarding raven will move a food cache when they suspect another raven knows where it is.[2]

---

1   Berkhof, Louis, *Systematic Theology* (Grand Rapids, Michigan / Cambridge, U. K.: Wm. B. Eerdmans Publishing 1996), 171.

2   Rozell, Ned, 'The Raven's Game of Hide and Seek,' Alaska Science Forum, February 3, 1999, http://www2.gi.alaska.edu/ScienceForum/ASF14/1426.html.

Ravens thrive in harsh environments by using their bird brains and bird skills to provide for themselves. Yet the Bible teaches that God feeds the ravens. 'Consider the ravens,' Jesus said. 'They neither sow nor reap, they have neither storehouse nor barn, and yet God feeds them' (Luke 12:24). '[God] gives to the beasts their food,' the psalmist wrote, 'and to the young ravens that cry' (Ps. 147:9). Ravens scavenge and hunt and spy and steal, and when they succeed it is God who provides for them.

This is an example of *concurrence*, the second aspect of divine providence. In concurrence, God works through natural means—ordinary cause-and-effect relationships—to carry out His plans for His creation. He 'cooperates with created things in every action, directing their distinctive properties to cause them to act as they do.'[3]

When I leave the lid on a garbage bin unfastened and a raven finds a stale crust inside, I have acted from my own absentminded nature, and the raven has acted from his instinct to scavenge, but standing behind this meal from scraps is God who orchestrated everything to provide for one of His creatures. The unguarded block of cheese in the back of the pickup truck? God provided this meal, too. Dumpsters, berry patches, road-kill, and even another raven's stockpile—all these are provided by God. In one sense, ravens eat because they find food using their own raven abilities. But in another sense, they receive their food from God's providential hand. He preserves their scavenging skills and controls the circumstances so they are fed.

What's more, ravens were instruments of God's providence when He fed the prophet Elijah. Do you know the story? God

---

3   Grudem, Wayne, *Systematic Theology: An Introduction to Biblical Doctrine* (Leicester, England: Inter-Varsity Press and Grand Rapids Michigan: Zondervan 1994), 317.

told Elijah to hide by the brook Cherith during a drought. 'You shall drink from the brook,' He said, 'and I have commanded the ravens to feed you there.' Elijah obeyed, and just as God promised, 'the ravens brought him bread and meat in the morning, and bread and meat in the evening ....' (1 Kings 17:1–6). When I was a child in Sunday School, my teacher taught us that when the ravens fed Elijah, God caused them to act contrary to their nature as ravens. But as I've observed ravens and learned more about their behavior, I've come to see this is an example of providential concurrence. God used the ravens' natural drive to scavenge food and hide their leftovers, and orchestrated the circumstances so they brought bread and meat to Elijah as he hid by the brook. Ravens did what ravens do, and in God's providence, Elijah was fed.

JOSEPH'S BROTHERS AND THE ASSYRIAN KING

As God accomplishes His plan in the world, He uses the actions of people, too. People act from their own desires, for their own reason, and according to their own natural human instincts, intellect, will, and strength, but they never act independently. They always do as God directs.

We can see the concurrence of God's will and human will throughout Scripture. Recall the Old Testament story of Joseph, for example. His brothers acted freely from their own jealous and murderous hearts when they sold him into slavery (Gen. 37:4, 11), but through their evil deed, God was accomplishing His plan to preserve His people. Joseph's brothers decided to sell him to the traders, and the traders decided to take him to Egypt, but at the same time, God *sent* him to Egypt (Gen. 45:4–8). God used the brothers' wicked intentions and actions 'to bring it about that many people should be kept alive ....' (Gen. 50:20). The brothers acted from their own dark desires, but they were never free of God's control. The brother's evil acts were orchestrated by God; they were means by which He worked His will. The whole story of Joseph—his father's favouritism, his brothers' hatred, his enslavement and rise to power—was controlled by God to accomplish His perfect plan. He directed everything so His people would survive during a seven-year famine that would come twenty years later. In His providence, God worked concurrently with human actions, even wicked ones, for His good purpose.

We find another example of concurrence later in the Old Testament when Isaiah prophesied that God would send the nation of Assyria against the nation of Israel (Isa. 10:5–19). Assyria, Isaiah said, would be an instrument in God's hands— the 'rod of God's anger' (verse 5). The people of Israel had been unfaithful to Him, and God planned to use the Assyrian army to execute His judgment on them for their wickedness. The king of Assyria would act from his own 'arrogant heart' to achieve his own selfish goals (verse 12), but God would be acting, too, using the king's wicked actions to accomplish His own wise purpose: the judgment of Israel. God would express His righteous wrath against their godlessness using the King of Assyria's evil desires and actions (verse 6). When it was all over, the king of Assyria would think he had destroyed Israel by himself (verses 7–11, 13–14)—and it *is* true that he would be acting for his own reasons, with his own power, and using his own strategy—but underneath it all and behind the scenes, God would be the ultimate cause of the king's action. In His providence, God would work concurrently with the acts of the King of Assyria and his army, using them as His instruments to accomplish His will.

WHATEVER HIS HAND AND HIS PLAN PREDESTINED

We also see concurrence in the central event of Scripture and history, the crucifixion of Christ. Peter explained how it worked in his sermon on Pentecost:

> Men of Israel, hear these words: Jesus of Nazareth, a man attested to you by God with mighty works and wonders and signs that God did through him in your midst, as you yourselves know—this Jesus, delivered up according to the definite plan and foreknowledge of God, you crucified and killed by the hands of lawless men. (Acts 2:22–23)

Jesus was crucified by the 'men of Israel,' together with 'lawless men'—the Roman officials and soldiers. But at the same time, God delivered Jesus up to be crucified. He planned the crucifixion, and He worked in people and events to make it happen.

Later, the believers in Jerusalem attributed Jesus' death to the actions of 'Herod and Pontius Pilate, along with the Gentiles and the peoples of Israel,' who had gathered in Jerusalem 'to do whatever [God's] hand and [His] plan had predestined to take place' (Acts 4:27-28). God planned the crucifixion of Jesus to save His people, but He carried out His plan through the actions of people who had their own reasons for doing what they did. The Jewish leaders hated Jesus so they wanted Him dead. Herod felt contempt for Him, so he had a bit of wicked fun at His expense. He dressed Jesus up in fine clothing to ridicule His claim to be a king, and sent Him, still dressed as a king, back to Pilate. And Pilate knew his own actions were unjust, but he handed Jesus over for crucifixion anyway because he wanted to please the Jews (Luke 23:22–24). Herod, Pontius Pilate, the Gentiles, and the leaders of Israel all had evil motives for their evil actions. And God used their wicked acts to accomplish redemption.

WHY DOES HE STILL FIND FAULT?

In the story of Joseph, the destruction of Israel by the Assyrians, and the crucifixion of Jesus, Scripture teaches the concurrence of God's will and human will. Even when people acted sinfully, they were doing what God planned for them to do. Despite these scriptural accounts of concurrence, some people reject the idea that a righteous God could ever will wicked human actions. If He did, they insist, He would be 'the author of sin'—a phrase that is used frequently, but as far as I know, never actually defined. Others accept that God worked this way in the specific cases of Joseph, the Assyrians, the crucifixion, and all the other cases in which Scripture clearly claims concurrence, but argue that these are extraordinary circumstances. This is not, they say, the way God ordinarily works.

I can understand why many people balk at the idea that God is *always* directing human actions. On the face of it, this would seem to leave no place for any genuine human choice and responsibility. If God orchestrates human actions, how can He hold people responsible for what they do?

But Ephesians 1:11 says God is working '*all* things after the counsel of his will' (emphasis mine). Besides the many examples of concurrence in its historical accounts, Scripture also teaches that human beings do not direct their own steps (Jer. 10:23), but God directs them (Prov. 16:9; Prov. 20:24). He directs human hearts, too (Ps. 105:25; Prov. 21:1; Phil. 2:13). It's clear from the witness of Scripture that concurrence is indeed the way God ordinarily works.

But how do we reconcile God's control over all circumstances, even the free acts of human beings, with real human choice and responsibility? How can God hold people responsible for wicked acts He planned for them to do? For wicked acts that serve His purposes? Scripture doesn't give us the complete answer to these questions, but it does give us some clues to how we might begin to answer them.

For starters, we know God is constantly restraining evil acts in the world (See Gen. 20:6, 1 Sam. 25:34, for instance). He chooses when to remove His restraint to allow people to do the wicked things their hearts already desire to do (Rom. 1:24, 26, 28). He brings about sinful human acts by taking away obstacles that keep people from acting on their sinful desires and then they do what they already wanted to do. God can bring about evil human acts without forcing anyone to do evil.

Let's use the King of Assyria's evil acts in the destruction of Israel to illustrate. Scripture says that God would send the king of Assyria against Israel as an instrument of His judgment. It also says the king would do what he already wanted to do (Isa. 10:7–11). God would accomplish His plan to destroy Israel by letting the Assyrian king act out his wicked desires. Afterwards, God would hold the king responsible for his acts because they were rooted in his own arrogant heart and boastful attitude (Isa. 10:12).

So even though wicked human acts accomplish God's plan, people are not puppets and God is not a puppet master. Our acts are the result of our own choices, and our choices are the result of our own attitudes and motives. When God accomplishes His plan by purposefully allowing specific evil acts, He intends for those acts to bring about results that are ultimately good. But when people do those same evil acts, they intend them for evil (Gen. 50:20). It is entirely right, then, for God to hold people accountable for their evil actions even though He planned for them to do them, because when they did them, they wanted to do evil.

Still, there is much about God's relationship to wicked human acts that we don't know. The bottom line is that Scripture teaches that God sovereignly controls human choices and actions, and also that people are responsible for their choices and actions. We can't deny either one even though we can't explain exactly how they fit together. We can't let our knowledge that as human beings we make real choices cause us to deny that God is always working in everything, including our choices. Nor, as Wayne Grudem reminds us, can we let the truth of God's sovereign control over 'all aspects of our lives,' including '[o]ur words, our steps, our movements, our hearts, and our abilities' cause us 'to deny the reality of our choices and actions .... We are significant and we are responsible. We *do have choices*, and these are real choices that bring about real results.'[4]

In the end, God's providential control of human choices and actions—choices and actions for which we are genuinely responsible—is one of the mysteries we affirm because God says it is so, and who are we 'to answer back to God?' (Rom. 9:20). And actually, that human actions and human hearts are both directed by God is not a truth to shrink from, but to embrace. How could God work all things together for good in our lives (Rom. 8:28) if He were not directing everything, including our own actions and the actions of people around us?

Who Is King? (Government)

> For God is the King of all the earth ....
> God reigns over the nations;
> God sits on his holy throne. (Ps. 47:7–8)

A third aspect of God's providence is His rule over creation. When we look at providence through the lens of God's *government*, we are focusing on His direction of all things *for His glory*. We touched a bit on this aspect of providence in the previous

---

4   Grudem, *Systematic Theology*, 321.

section on concurrence, because the two categories overlap, but concurrence highlights God's providential means—or the *way* He works in everything—and His government highlights His providential ends—or the *goal* He is achieving. As king of the universe, God has a decree, and His decree has a final goal: His own glory. He is always working in the universe to achieve this goal. He is exerting His rule in order to reveal His glory.

As the king of the universe, God appoints all other kings, rulers, governments and powers, and they are all subject to Him (1 Pet. 2:14; Rom. 13:1–2). He establishes every kingdom, empire, and nation, and destroys each one when its 'allotted period' is up (Acts 17:26). As the ruler of all creation, God brought Nebuchadnezzar, the arrogant and powerful King of Babylon, down to nothing, and He kept him there until Nebuchadnezzar finally recognized God's rule and gave praise and honor to Him alone. Eventually Nebuchadnezzar acknowledged that God 'does according to his will among the host of heaven and among the inhabitants of the earth,' and no one, not even the most powerful ruler in the world, 'can stay his hand' (Dan. 4:34–35). Eventually, God's rule will result in the destruction of 'every rule and every authority and power,' and His absolute rule will be established forever (1 Cor. 15:24–28). Everyone—kings, rulers, and powers included—will finally acknowledge that He is 'King of kings and Lord of lords' (1 Tim. 6:15). God will achieve His ultimate goal when all people and all powers confess how glorious He is.

Paul's statement in Romans 11:36 is the perfect summary of God's works of creation and providence. He writes, 'For from him and through him and to him are all things. To him be glory forever.' Everything is 'from him,' because He created it all. Everything is 'through him,' because He preserves it all and works in it all. And as He governs everything, He ensures that He

Himself—His *glory*—is the final goal of everything. So because God rules, all things are 'to him.' Because He rules, '*to him be glory forever.*'

Working as One

> ... men spoke from God as they were carried along by the Holy Spirit. (2 Pet. 1:21)

God's works of providence, like His works of creation, are accomplished by all three persons of the Trinity. Just as the Son was the Father's agent in the creation of the universe, He is also the Father's agent in the preservation of the universe. The Son upholds everything He created. He is constantly working to hold all things together (Heb. 1:3; Col. 1:17). The Spirit is also active in the preservation of creation. He works to maintain the physical life of God's creatures. You are alive right now only because the Spirit continues to give you life (Job 34:14–15).

The Spirit also works within people to cause them to do the good works God wills for them to do. For instance, the Spirit guided the authors of Scripture to the truth (John 16:13), and then 'carried [them] along' as they wrote down this truth (2 Pet. 1:21). The Bible's authors searched their own memories, processed their own thoughts, and wrote the text in their own words, but at the same time, the Spirit was working within them, making sure they wrote what God intended for them to write. The final product, then, is truly their own work, but also truly God's work—and truly the *Word of God*. This work of the Spirit is an example of providential concurrence. God executed His plan to reveal Himself and His works to His people through the agency of the Spirit, who worked in the thoughts and actions of the apostles and prophets.

The prayers of believers are another example of providential concurrence worked by the Spirit. We pray using our own word for the matters that concern us, but at the same time, the Spirit is working within us to make our prayers consistent with God's will. And when God answers our Spirit-worked prayers, they become, in turn, one of the means through which He works to fulfill His purposes in our lives and in the world (James 5:16).

For His Glory Is Also for Our Good

[W]e know that for those who love God all things work together for good .... (Rom. 8:28)

Let's return to where we started this chapter, to the question of how an understanding of God's providence benefits us. How does it help for us to know that God is working in everything that happens, including terrible tragedies and evil acts of evil people, to accomplish His plan?

For one, if we know that God planned and works all the events and circumstances of our lives, we also know everything that happens to us has a purpose. Nothing—not even tragedies— are meaningless because God has reasons for them. No suffering is gratuitous, because no suffering comes to us by chance, but rather, all suffering comes from His plan.

Without an understanding of providence, the only answer we can give to the question of why Christians suffer is the one a guest speaker at my church once gave. 'We suffer,' he said, 'because we live in a fallen world.' This was his whole answer, and, he said, the only answer anyone could give. And his statement is true—as far as it goes. The world we live in is a cursed one, and the curse brings suffering with it. But is this answer enough to help someone maintain hope in the midst of a trial? Does it give meaning to suffering?

While my husband was sick with cancer, knowing we weren't suffering simply because we lived in a fallen world, but also (and more importantly) because our good God had specific purposes for our suffering was a great comfort to us. Our suffering was not just the bad luck of the draw, but was specifically chosen for us by God, who loved us, and who was using our trials for His glory and our good. Our suffering was not meaningless misfortune; it was given to us by our good God for His good reasons. When my husband eventually passed away, knowing my grief was not in vain because it was accomplishing God's perfect purpose helped me face my future as a widow and single parent.

We will never know all of God's reasons for any particular difficult circumstance, but those who trust Him can rest in the knowledge that He has wise reasons for everything He does. And we *can* know God's ultimate purpose for every single one of our trials: His own glory (Rom. 11:36, Eph. 1:11–12). He is showing us more of who He is through the difficult circumstances of our lives.

There's another universal purpose for trials in the life of a believer. All our trials are working to make us like Christ (Rom. 8:28–29). Our God is a kind Father, and the trials He gives us are instruments He uses to make us holy. They are His discipline, and yes, 'painful rather than pleasant,' but over time, they will 'yield the peaceful fruit of righteousness' (Heb. 12:5–11).

Our suffering also forms a mature and enduring faith within us. I am less afraid of the future now than I was before my husband's illness and death. I know that in His mercy, in our most difficult circumstances, God helped me and my children, giving us an income to provide for us, and sending people to comfort us. When I needed to accomplish tasks that had previously been my husband's responsibility—tasks that seemed impossible to me—God gave me the strength and wisdom to do them. God was faithful during my long, dark trial, so I know He will also carry me through any future difficulties. My experience taught me that when we understand that our trials work to strengthen our faith, and when we actually experience them working this way, we find deep joy even in suffering (James 1:2–4).

Can you see that for the believer, trials are actually a benefit of salvation? God uses our suffering to discipline us *because* we are His children (Heb. 12:7–8). He is using our trials to transform us, and as He does, He makes our final salvation certain. Knowing some of God's reasons for our suffering doesn't make our trials easy, but it does give us courage to endure them, and hope for our future.

Understanding God's providence gives us confidence that He will always care for us. If He provides prey for ravens, He will provide everything we need, too. We are, after all, worth more to Him than any bird (Matt. 6:25–26). We will still need to work to provide for ourselves (the ravens, remember, hunt their own prey), but underneath everything we acquire for ourselves is God's provision for us. When we are anxious about the things we don't have, we are doubting God's willingness and ability to provide everything we actually need, and everything truly good for us. When we are not content with what God has supplied for us, we show our lack of trust in His wisdom and goodness.

When we understand the providence of God, we will thank Him for everything: the obviously significant things He works, like healed diseases and dream jobs; and also the small everyday pleasures He gives, like the smell of fresh bread or warm water for baths. But being thankful for the pleasant gifts God gives isn't enough. The apostle Paul exhorts us to be thankful 'in *all* circumstances' (1 Thess. 5:18, emphasis mine). And standing underneath genuine thanksgiving in difficult times is a true understanding of the doctrine of providence. God's children can be thankful in everything because even in our trials, God is caring for us, and even when we suffer, He is accomplishing His good purpose for us. And in all His works of providence—the big gifts and small ones, and our trials, too—God is blessing us by revealing His glory to us. 'To him be all glory forever and ever.'

Prayer

God of providence,

Thank you for your constant care for your creation, and your constant care for me. Thank you for giving me life, for preserving my life, and for accomplishing your purposes in it. Thank you for the comfort and hope that comes from knowing everything that happens in my life and in the world comes from your providential hand.

When I face difficult circumstances, remind me that they come from you, and are working for my good and for your glory. Reveal yourself to me through all your providential works.

QUESTIONS

HE UPHOLDS THE UNIVERSE

God didn't create the universe and then leave it to run on its own. He is always working in it to preserve it, to unfold His plan in it, and to achieve His purpose for it. Even the difficult circumstances in our lives come from His hand, and He is using them to accomplish His purposes. While we don't understand all of God's purposes for any particular circumstance, we do know His ultimate purpose for everything He does: His own glory. He is revealing Himself in all His works of providence.

1. What people has God used as agents of His providential care for you today? Have you thanked Him for them?

2. What does the doctrine of providence teach us about the laws of nature? What is the relationship, for instance, between God's providence and the law of gravity?

3. What is God's relationship to the leaders who govern us? What should our attitude toward our leaders be? (See Rom. 13:1–7 and 1 Pet. 2:13–17).

4. Do you worry about the future? What truths about the providence of God might ease your worry?

5. For each believer, what is the final result of God's providential care? Is the outcome of His providence different for unbelievers?

6. Can you thank God for the times of suffering He has brought into your life? If so, why are you thankful? If not, why not?

Chapter 9

He Saves

Do you remember the story of the forbidden tree in the Garden of Eden? God created trees in the garden, 'every tree that is pleasant to the sight and good for food' (Gen. 2:9). And in the middle of the garden He put two special trees—the tree of life, and the tree of the knowledge of good and evil. 'You may surely eat of every tree of the garden,' God told Adam, the first man, 'but of the tree of the knowledge of good and evil you shall not eat, for in the day that you eat of it you shall surely die' (Gen. 2:16–17).

While I was on vacation a few years ago, I attended a Bible study in a local church in the town I was visiting. The text for the night was the second chapter of Genesis, which includes these instructions from God to Adam about the fruit from the trees in the Garden of Eden. The story of Adam's response to God's command comes in the next chapter, so the teacher didn't mention it in this session of the Bible study, but anyone acquainted with the big story of the Bible knows what happened. Adam disobeyed God and ate the one fruit God told him not to eat. With his one act of disobedience, everything changed— for him, for his wife Eve, and for us, too. Adam, the first man, represented the whole human race, and when he disobeyed God, his disobedience was charged to him, and also to every other human who would ever live. God cursed Adam for his disobedience, and along with Adam, He cursed every person Adam represented. In Adam's one rebellious act, the relationship between God and all humankind was broken. God became estranged from us, or to put it another way, we became objects of His wrath (Eph. 2:3). All humankind became 'hostile to God' (Rom. 8:7), too. And it all started with that one forbidden tree.

During the discussion at the end of the Bible study, one woman asked a question. 'Why,' she said, 'would God put that tree in the garden?'

It's a good question, isn't it? Every tree was good for food but one. The presence of this single prohibited tree among all the permitted ones brought misery to all creation. Later we learn God took powerful precautions to prevent the consequences that would follow if Adam and Eve ate from the tree of life. If they had eaten from it after they ate the forbidden fruit, they would have lived forever in their sinful state. So God placed cherubim and a flaming sword to keep them away (Gen. 3:24). Why didn't He do the same thing with the tree of the knowledge of good and evil? Or, better yet, as the woman suggested, why didn't He just not create that one dangerous tree in the first place?

The teacher turned the question back to the class for discussion: *Why did God put a forbidden tree in the garden?* No one volunteered an answer, so he began asking individual students directly. Still no one answered. Eventually the teacher directed the question to me. I considered saying I didn't know, but the truth is, I'd thought about this question and I had an answer. I knew not everyone would agree with me, but I can't resist a good discussion, so I replied, 'I think God planned from the beginning for humankind to fall, and He put the tree of the knowledge of good and evil in place to be the way for it to happen.'

I remember the teacher's response perfectly. 'That,' he said, 'is *twisted* theology!'

I hadn't expected him to be so direct, but I understood the reason for it. I received his public rebuke because the idea that God would be involved in the fall by purposefully placing a tree as the means to accomplish it was offensive to him. And he isn't alone. Many people are troubled by the thought that God planned for humankind to fall, and even more troubled by the thought that He placed a forbidden tree in the garden so it would happen.

Twisted Theology or Glorious Plan?

> In him we have obtained an inheritance, having been predestined according to the purpose of him who works all things according to the counsel of his will …. (Eph. 1:11)

As we study God's work of salvation, I hope you will see that for the triune God to make an eternal plan for Father, Son, and Spirit to save fallen people, and then bring everything in this plan to pass, including the fall of humankind, is not twisted, but exactly right. I hope you will understand that through His saving plan and saving work, our God is revealed in all His glory, and that the revelation of the glory of God is a perfect reason to put the means to the fall in the middle of the home He created for the first human beings.

In Ephesians 1, the apostle Paul gave an overview of God's whole plan to save.

> Blessed be the God and Father of our Lord Jesus Christ, who has blessed us in Christ with every spiritual blessing in the heavenly places, even as he chose us in him *before the foundation* of the world, that we should be holy and blameless before him. In love he predestined us for adoption as sons through Jesus Christ, according to the purpose of his will, to the praise of his glorious grace, with which he has blessed us in the Beloved. In him we have *redemption through his blood*, the forgiveness of our trespasses, according to the riches of his grace, which he lavished upon us, in all wisdom and insight making known to us the mystery of his will, according to his purpose, which he set forth in Christ as a *plan for the fullness of time*, to unite all things in him, things in heaven and things on earth.
>
> In him we have obtained an inheritance, having been predestined according to the purpose of him who works *all things* according to the counsel of his will, so that we who were the first to hope in Christ might be to the praise of his glory. In him you also, when you heard the word of truth, the gospel of your salvation, and believed in him, were sealed with the promised Holy Spirit, who is the guarantee of our inheritance until we acquire possession of it, to the praise of his glory. (Eph. 1:3–14, emphasis mine)

God's big plan for creation, a plan formed before He created anything (verse 4), was to unite everything in Christ (verses 9-10). How would He accomplish this? By 'redemption through [Christ's] blood, the forgiveness of our trespasses' (verse 7). From the beginning, God planned to save people for Himself (verse 4) by sending Christ into the world to die for them, and then sending the Spirit into the world to guarantee they actually receive their inheritance (verses 13–14). From eternity, before creation, God planned to reconcile sinners to Himself. His plan to redeem fallen humanity was not a contingency plan made *in case* people sinned. It was His plan A.

It's in the context of God's plan to redeem sinners by forgiving their sins that Paul said God works *all things* according to His plan (verse 11). Every single piece of the story of God's salvation is in the *all things* He works. This includes the fall of humankind, and, as the means to the fall, the placement of the tree of the knowledge of good and evil. Both were prerequisites to His goal to unite everything in Christ. If God was going to reconcile sinners to Himself, there needed to be sinners to reconcile.

What else can we learn about God's eternal plan of redemption from this passage in Ephesians? For one, since His plan to save was made before the foundation of the world when nothing existed but God Himself, we know it was not influenced by anyone or anything in creation. He made an independent choice to redeem human creatures. Second, these verses explain what it was in God that moved Him to save sinners. He decided to redeem people because of His love. '[I]n love' He chose people to redeem (verse 5), and 'from the riches of His grace' He accomplished His plan to redeem them (verses 7–10). And third, while the eternal well-being of those who are being saved is one of the purposes for God's saving work, His highest goal is 'the praise of his glorious grace' (verse 6). He chose to save sinners to show how glorious His grace is.

Finally, this passage teaches that the divine plan to save includes all three members of the Trinity. The Father, Son, and Spirit agreed to the plan in eternity, and then, in history, each one voluntarily carried out His role. The Father directed the plan (verses 4-5, 10–11). The Son carried out His part of the plan by accomplishing redemption (verses 7–9). And the Spirit fulfilled His mission by coming to apply the redemption accomplished by the Son (verses 13–14).

Planned and Directed by the Father

> [W]hen the fullness of time had come, God sent forth his Son
> ... to redeem those who were under the law.... (Gal. 4:4–5)

The Father is the architect of the Triune God's plan to save. 'Before the foundation of the world,' He planned to send the Son to accomplish salvation (1 Pet. 1:20). He predetermined all the details of the Son's atoning death (Acts 2:23; 4:27–28). In eternity past, He chose the sinners to be saved (Rom. 8:29–30; Eph. 1:4; 1 Pet. 1:1–2).

Then, in time and history, He directed—and is directing—all things to ensure His plan is accomplished. He gave the ones He chose to save to the Son (John 6:37–40; 10:27–29), and sent the Son into the world to redeem them (Gal. 4:4; Rom. 8:32). He coordinated both the incarnation and the crucifixion. The Father prepared a body for the Son (Heb. 10:5), and orchestrated the events of His atoning death (Acts 4:27–28). He 'put [Jesus] forward as a propitiation' (Rom. 3:25). The Father counted our sins to Him, so that when Jesus died, He bore the punishment for our sins in our place (2 Cor. 5:21). The Father exacted the just punishment for sin on His sin-bearing Son, and accepted the

Son's sacrifice on our behalf. When the Son's atoning work was done, the Father raised Him from the dead (Acts 2:24; 5:30; 13:30), took Him into heaven (Acts 1:9–11) and seated Him at His own right hand (Acts 5:31). And it is the Father who, on the basis of the Son's sacrifice, forgives sinners and declares them righteous (Rom. 8:33).

The Father, together with the Son, sent the Spirit into the world (John 14:16–17; 15:26) to apply the Son's finished work to those God chose to save. He sent the Spirit to live in every believer, ensuring their final salvation (2 Cor. 1:20–22) and enabling them to proclaim the gospel (John 15:26).

Finally, it is the Father who will restore creation. He cursed it after the fall (Rom. 8:20), so now nothing in the universe works the way it is supposed to work. Chickweed grows thick in my garden and threatens to strangle the vegetables I'm trying to grow for food. Our homes are susceptible to mold and rot, and our favorite shade trees die and need to be cut down. And eventually we will all die, too. But the Father, who 'subjected [creation] to futility' in the first place, will set it all 'free from its bondage to corruption' in the end (Rom. 8:20–21). He will restore everything when He creates a new heavens and new earth (Rev. 21:1–4). Once again, creation will work the way it did before the fall. There will be no more choking weeds, rotting porches, dead trees, or dying people for all of the never-ending future.

Since the Father planned and directed the work of salvation, Scripture says salvation is *from* Him (1 Cor. 1:30; 2 Cor. 5:18). Yes, the Son did the work that reconciled the Father to sinful humanity, but He was working as an agent of the Father. The Father was 'reconciling the world to himself' in Christ (2 Cor. 5:18–19) and now He is blessing us 'in Christ with every spiritual blessing' (Eph. 1:3). The apostle Paul thanked the Father for salvation (Col. 1:12) because He orchestrated it. Without the Father's planning and sending, no one could be saved.

Accomplished by the Son

> [T]here is one mediator between God and men, the man Christ Jesus, who gave himself as a ransom for all, which is the testimony given at the proper time. (1 Tim. 2:5–6)

When the time was right according to the Father's plan, the Son came to be the 'one *mediator* between God and men' (1 Tim. 2:5). He fulfilled His role in salvation by coming into our world to make peace between God and sinful humanity. Adam ate the forbidden fruit, remember, and since then, we are all born into estrangement: God is alienated from humanity and humanity is alienated from God. Every person inherited guilt and corruption from Adam, so every person is born under God's wrath. And in turn, our corruption makes us hostile to Him.

This is why we needed a mediator. A mediator is someone who represents the interests of both parties in a dispute and works out an agreement—or *reconciliation*—between them. To do his job, a mediator must be able identify with both parties and see the contentious issues from both viewpoints.

The Son, who was already God, and already identified with the divine side of the conflict between God and humankind, became the perfect mediator in His incarnation. He remained divine, but added a human nature. He became a genuine human being and lived a genuine human life, subject to all the weaknesses of true humanity. Like every other human, He grew tired, He became hungry, and He felt pain. The eternal Son of God voluntarily identified with humanity because only someone who was both truly God and truly human could be the mediator in the conflict between God and human sinners. Only 'the man Christ Jesus' could represent God to us and us to God.

When a mediator reconciles the two sides in human disagreements, there is usually fault on each side. Both sides will have valid complaints, so both sides must make amends for the wrongs they have done before the two sides can come to an agreement. But in the broken relationship between God and sinners, all the wrong-doing comes from one side—the human one. We have rebelled against the God who created us and sustains us. Instead of living for His glory, we live for ourselves. Instead of loving Him more than we love anything else, we love created things, like our possessions, our family, or our friends more than we love Him.

God's enmity toward us, then, is perfectly justified. It is His righteous response to our rebellion against Him. Our enmity toward God, on the other hand, is completely unjustified. We have no legitimate reason to be hostile to Him. He has never wronged us. (Actually, our unjustified hostility toward Him is yet more rebellion against Him. It is one more valid reason for His wrath toward us.)

In the dispute between God and sinners, the sinner's side is the only one that needs to made amends. We need to set things right with God. But even if we wanted to—and because of our hostility to God, we *don't* want to—we couldn't undo our offences. And God can't simply withhold His righteous response to our sins, either. He can't decide to look the other way or sweep our sins under a rug, because He always does what is right. He can't just 'get over' His wrath, because as the perfect judge, He must always execute justice, and His wrath is the proper judicial sentence for our crimes. The two sides in this conflict, then, are at an impasse. There is no way forward—or so it would seem.

But the mediator in this dispute isn't an ordinary mediator. We can't make amends for our offences against God, but the incarnate Son can make amends to God on our behalf.

And this is exactly what He did. He died on the cross to bear the wrath of God that we, with our many offences, deserved. He substituted Himself for every believer and absorbed God's wrath against them. The Bible calls what Christ's death did for us *propitiation* because on the basis of His death in our place, God's wrath toward us was satisfied. His wrath was appeased—or *propitiated*—in the death of His Son.

DOUBLE-SIDED OBEDIENCE

Theologians also call what the Son did as He endured the just penalty for our sin on our behalf His *passive obedience*. This term uses the word *passive* in a way that's unusual for us now. It doesn't mean the Son didn't actively participate in His own death. We know He did. He voluntarily and purposefully gave up His life (John 10:18). No, in this case, the word *passive* refers to the *suffering* involved in His enduring the penalty for us. (We use the root *pass* in the same way when we speak of Christ's suffering and death as His *passion*.)

The Son's suffering was *obedience* because as He surrendered to the leaders who took Him away to crucify Him, as He bore His own cross and stumbled to Calvary, and as He gave up His life, He was doing His Father's will. He drank 'the cup that the Father had given [Him]' (John 18:11). He was '*obedient* to the point of death, even death on a cross' (Phil. 2:8, emphasis mine).

The Son's passive obedience is the basis for God's forgiveness of our sin. Adam, the first man, represented the whole human race when he disobeyed God and ate from the forbidden tree. God condemned the whole human race because of his representative disobedience. The incarnate Son, the man Christ

Jesus, represented others, too. The sins of His people were placed on Him and He endured God's judicial sentence in their place. God pardons sinners because of the Son's representative passive obedience (Rom. 5:12–15).

Are you a believer? Then the Son *substituted* Himself for you and bore the legal *penalty* for your sin, and so God has pardoned you. This is why we also call Christ's atonement *penal substitution*. Your sins were forgiven because God's wrath against you, which was the just penalty for your sin, was satisfied when Jesus died in your place.

The incarnate Son represented you in another way, too. He also lived a perfectly obedient life in your place. Why did you need Him to do this? Because God's standards for us have requirements we must fulfill. We need a perfect record of obedience to every one of God's rules. I haven't obeyed God perfectly, so my own record won't work for me—and yours won't work for you either. We all need Jesus' life of perfect obedience to God's requirements counted as ours. His life-long obedience to all of God's rules for humankind, or His *active obedience*, is as crucial to our salvation as His penalty-bearing death. No one can be declared righteous unless they are 'found in [Christ], not having a righteousness of [their] own that comes from the law, but that which comes through faith in Christ ...' (Phil. 3:9). Thankfully, God credits Christ's active obedience to everyone who has faith. If you believe, 'you are in Christ Jesus, who became to us ... *righteousness*' (1 Cor. 1:30–31, emphasis mine). His righteous record—His active obedience—is counted to you, and you are counted righteous in Him.

Both the passive and active obedience of Christ Jesus provide the grounds for the believer's justification. For God to declare us righteous, we need the Son to represent us in both His death and His life, and this is exactly what He came to do for all those the Father gave Him. We are declared righteous—or we are *justified*—based on the Son's obedient life and atoning death, which we receive by faith. This is what justification *by faith* is: justification based on Christ's work alone, both His passive and active obedience, received by faith.

A DONE DEAL

When the incarnate Son's atoning work was finished, God resurrected Him. He had paid for sin, so '[I]t was impossible for him not to rise from the dead, because he himself was sinless, and death has no claim to, or hold upon, sinless people.'[1] Do you believe? Then the resurrection of the Son is the guarantee that all of your sins are paid for and you are forgiven.

Shortly after His resurrection, the Son ascended into heaven, where He 'always lives to make intercession' for those who belong to Him. If you are a believer, the incarnate Son is in heaven with the Father interceding for you right now, and He will continue to intercede until you—and all the rest of those the Father gave Him—are judged righteous in the final judgment. The atoning work Jesus did for you will succeed for sure because as the resurrected God-man, He sits at the right hand of the Father and advocates for you (Heb. 7:25; Rom. 8:34).

When God makes His final declaration that you are righteous, it will be because God's Son came for you, lived for you, died for you, and then ascended to heaven to intercede for you. He accomplished your salvation. Without His work, no one could be saved.

---

1   Sproul, R. C., *Truths We Confess: A Layman's Guide to the Westminster Confession of Faith,* Vol. 1, *The Triune God* (Phillipsburg, New Jersey: P & R Publishing 2006), 253.

Applied by the Spirit

> [Y]ou … were sealed with the promised Holy Spirit, who is
> the guarantee of our inheritance until we acquire possession of
> it … (Eph. 1:13–14)

As we've just seen, the Son's work solves God's side of the
dispute between God and sinners. For those the Father chose
in eternity past and gave to the Son to save, God's wrath has
been propitiated. In Christ, God has been reconciled to them.
And this reconciliation comes with a message—an invitation for
them to 'be reconciled to God' (2 Cor. 5:18–20).

But when sinners hear the good news of the gospel with its
invitation to be reconciled to God, their natural response is still
hostility toward Him (Rom. 8:7). Sinners need to have God's
wrath toward them satisfied, and they also need to have their
own opposition to God removed.

Removing the sinner's hostility to God is the work of the
Spirit. The Spirit applies the accomplished work of the Son to
the people God chose to save, and then changes them from the
inside out. He turns their opposition to God into love for Him.
We call this initial change worked by the Spirit in a sinner's
heart *regeneration*, or *being born again*. We are all born spiritually
dead, and just as a physically dead person can't respond when
called, a spiritually dead person can't respond to God's call to be
reconciled to Him. She must be raised to spiritual life first. Our
natural human condition is 'dead in trespasses and sins' and the
only solution to this kind of deadness is to be born again—to be
made 'alive together with Christ' (Eph. 2:1–5). The Spirit must
breathe spiritual life into our dead hearts, and then we can be—
and *are*—reconciled to God. Through the power of the Spirit
and His regenerative work, our hostility to God disappears. We

begin to understand the message of the gospel, and we respond positively to it.

I've already told some of the story of my own rebirth. When I was a child, I listened to a sermon on Christ's death and understood that I was a sinner and needed what was accomplished there. This could only happen because the Spirit had regenerated me. He removed my natural hostility to God so I could see the beauty of the cross. I understood that God's invitation to reconciliation was good news because the Spirit had raised me to spiritual life. I responded to the sermon with faith in Christ because I had been born again.

Even the faith by which I trusted in the Son's work, then, was God's gift to me (Phil. 1:29 and Eph. 2:8). Yes, my faith was my own, but it was the result of the Spirit's regenerating work within me. And it is the same for every believer, even those who are not aware of the moment they began to believe. When we are born again by the Spirit, we begin to see the work of the Son as our only hope, and God's message of reconciliation as truly good news. We see the glory of the gospel and we embrace it. A positive response to the gospel of salvation is caused by the Spirit's gracious work, so it is truly by *grace* we are saved through faith.

FRUIT PRODUCTION

The Spirit doesn't regenerate us and then leave, but He continues to live inside every believer. His inner work produces a desire to please God and a willingness to serve Him. He causes us to want to be holy as God is holy. And along with the desire to be righteous, the Spirit also gives us the power to be righteous. God, through the agency of the Spirit, works within us to cause us 'both to will and to work for his good pleasure' (Phil. 2:13).

The Spirit accomplishes our regeneration in an instant, but His work producing holiness within us is a lifelong process. We grow in holiness over time as the Spirit gives us the desire and ability to extinguish sin in our lives (Rom. 8:13). And unlike our regeneration, which is a work of the Spirit alone, our growth in holiness is a cooperative work. The Spirit works within us and we work, too. As we 'walk by the Spirit' we crucify 'the flesh with its passions and desires' (Gal. 5:16, 24). Through the Spirit's power, we begin to have victory over sin. Our victory over sin won't be complete in this life, but the war has begun, and in the Spirit, we will win more and more of our battles.

And as we kill our sin by the power of the Spirit, He also produces Christ-like qualities—or 'the fruit of the Spirit'—within us. As the Spirit works, our 'love, joy, peace, patience, kindness, goodness, faithfulness, gentleness, [and] self-control' increases (Gal. 5:22–23). Can you see this spiritual fruit growing in your own life? Are you more patient than you were? If God doesn't provide what you ask for immediately, are you more willing to wait for it? Are you more willing to do without it altogether if His answer is *no*? Has your love increased? Do you have more genuine concern for the welfare of others than you did before you believed? Do you have peace with God? Can you approach Him with confidence when you need His help? Believers can expect to continue to develop the fruit of the Spirit throughout their lives. As the indwelling Spirit shows us what Christ is like, we grow more like Him. As we '[behold] the glory of the Lord,' we are changed 'from one degree of glory to another' (2 Cor. 3:16–18).

The Spirit also works within us to assure that we are God's own adopted children (Rom. 8:15–16). Are you confident that as a father to you, God will always treat you kindly? Do you come to Him for help, sure that He will help? Your assurance that God is your loving father is the work of the Spirit. The presence of the Spirit within us also guarantees that we will receive our final inheritance—eternal life with our adopted Father—because the Spirit's power will keep us faithful until the end (Eph. 1:13–14).

Aren't you thankful for the Spirit's work within you? Right now, He is working to make you holy. Right now, He is keeping you faithful. Without the work of the Spirit, you could not be saved. Without His work, no one could be saved.

Revealing the Trinity to Us

> For through him we both have access in one Spirit to the Father.
> (Eph. 2:18)

As we've seen, salvation is a triune work. The Father, Son, and Spirit each agreed to fulfill a specific role in God's work of salvation. The specific role of each person is voluntary, but it is not arbitrary. Like God's works of creation and providence, which are intended to reveal Him to us, His work of salvation is intended to reveal Him, too.[2] The specific roles of Father, Son, and Spirit in salvation are intended to give us a glimpse into the life of the three persons of the Trinity as they are in eternity. The internal relations of the persons of the Trinity in eternity, then, give shape to their roles in God's work of salvation.

The Father's role in salvation—His planning and directing—is an extension of His eternal relationship to the Son and the Spirit.[3] The Father, remember, eternally generates the Son. The Son is *from* Him. The Spirit eternally proceeds from the Father and the Son, so the Spirit is *from* both the Father and the Son. But the Father is eternally from no one. It is exactly right, then,

---

2   Sanders, Fred, *The Deep Things of God: How the Trinity Changes Everything* (Wheaton, Illinois: Crossway 2010), 133.

3   Sanders, Fred, *The Deep Things of God: How the Trinity Changes Everything*, 155.

for the Father to be the source and sender in the triune work of salvation.

The Son, as the eternal Son of the Father, voluntarily came into the world as an agent of the Father to execute His plan to save. His role in salvation brings 'the relationship of divine sonship [which] has always existed as part of the very definition of God' into our world—'into created reality and human history.'[4]

And the Spirit? He eternally proceeds from both the Father and the Son, and as He does the will of the Father and the Son by applying the salvation accomplished through the Son's work, 'His eternal relationship with the Father and the Son begins to take place among us.'[5]

Not Twisted, But Gloriously Perfect

> In him you also, when you heard the word of truth, the gospel of
> your salvation, and believed in him, were sealed with the promised
> Holy Spirit ... to the praise of his glory. (Eph. 1:13–14)

Like the Bible study teacher in the story at the beginning of this chapter, do you struggle with the truth that God planned for the people He would create to fall into sin? That He planned for them to need Him to save them?

It may help to consider all the results of God's work of salvation. What besides—and *greater* than—the salvation of sinners is accomplished? For one, as we've just discussed, through His work of salvation, the triune nature of God is revealed to us. God sent the second person of the Trinity, His Son, into the world to save sinners, and with the revelation of the Son, we begin to see that the one God who created everything is not a single-person God, but Father and Son. And when the Father and Son sent the

---

4   Sanders, Fred, *The Deep Things of God: How the Trinity Changes Everything*, 155.

5   Sanders, Fred, *The Deep Things of God: How the Trinity Changes Everything*, 155.

Spirit into the world to aid in the spread of the good news of salvation and to apply the salvation accomplished by the Son to the sinners God intended to save, the third person of the Trinity is revealed. What was only hinted at apart from God's work of salvation is revealed to us in it.

Could God have revealed Himself as the three-person God in another way? If humanity hadn't fallen and hadn't needed to be saved, would we know the Father, Son, and Spirit? I don't know, but I do know that in God's eternal plan, He decided to reveal His eternal triune nature to us by saving sinners.

Let's add to our list of praiseworthy results achieved by God's work of redemption. Because God saved sinners, we've seen the cross, the ultimate display of His justice, love, mercy, and wisdom. Because God saved sinners, we know how great His grace is (Eph. 1:6; 2:7). Because God saved sinners, every knee will bow before Jesus Christ and every tongue will confess that He is Lord, and the Father will be glorified (Phil. 2:9–11).

The forbidden tree placed by God in the midst of the Garden of Eden brought disaster for sure, but disaster isn't the end of the story. The end of the story, and the point of it, is God's revelation of Himself. Through God's redeeming work, we can know Him: We learn He is Father, Son, and Spirit; we see His justice, love, wisdom, and more. That God planned in eternity to save His human creatures, and that His plan included every detail of the salvation story, including the way His human creatures would fall into sin, ensures that the ultimate accomplishment of His work of salvation is exactly what it should be: His own glory.

Prayer

God who saves,

I know I am a sinner. I know I cannot save Himself. I need the forgiveness that comes only through Christ's death. I need

Christ's perfect obedience counted as mine so I can be counted righteous. I need the new birth worked by the Spirit, because without it, I would never believe.

Thank you, Father, for loving me before the foundation of the world, and for sending your Son to redeem me. Thank you for sending the Spirit to keep me faithful until I finally inherit eternity with you. And thank you for showing me your glory through your triune work of salvation.

QUESTIONS

HE SAVES

Before God created the world, He planned to accomplish salvation in it. In eternity past, the Father chose people to save, the Son agreed to come into the world to save them, and the Spirit agreed to apply the Son's accomplished salvation to them. In history and time, Father, Son, and Spirit are working out this divine plan to save, with each one fulfilling His role. And through this triune work of salvation, the perfection of our triune God is revealed to us.

1. Read Romans 8:26–34. According to this passage, what is the role of the Father in your salvation? What is the role of the Son? The Spirit?

2. Why does Scripture say salvation is *from* the Father?

3. What qualifies the incarnate Son to be the mediator between God and humankind?

4. What is the difference between the Son's active obedience and His passive obedience? Why are both necessary for sinners to be justified?

5. Shortly before he died, theologian J. Gresham Machen sent a telegram to his friend John Murray. 'I'm so thankful,' it said, 'for the active obedience of Christ. No hope without it.'[6] Why would the doctrine of Christ's active obedience give hope to a dying believer?

---

6   De Jong, Brian L., 'What Machen Meant,' The Orthodox Presbyterian Church Webpage, https://www.opc.org/nh.html?article_id=383 .

6. Find one text of Scripture you could use to defend the teaching that Christ's death is *penal substitution*? That it is *propitiation*?

7. What is the Son's role in God's work of salvation right now? Why is this work significant?

8. Make a list of things the Son has done to accomplish your salvation. Thank God for each one.

9. Do you see evidence the Holy Spirit is working in you to make you holy? Do you see the fruit of the Spirit listed in Galatians 5:22–23 in your life?

10. List three goals God intends to accomplish through His work of salvation. What is the ultimate goal of His saving work? What texts from Scripture could you use to support your answers?

Conclusion

The First Question

A group of friends were riding horseback in the rugged bush of the Rocky Mountains. After climbing for a couple of hours, they came to a ridge that overlooked an untouched mountain pasture, and they all held their horses to take in the spectacular view. An emerald lake lay below them, and on the other side of the valley, more craggy glacier-topped mountains.

One of the riders began to sing, and one by one the others joined him until they became a full-voiced choir:

> O Lord my God, When I in awesome wonder,
> Consider all the worlds Thy Hands have made;
> I see the stars, I hear the rolling thunder,
> Thy power throughout the universe displayed.
>
> Then sings my soul, My Savior God, to Thee,
> How great Thou art, How great Thou art.
> Then sings my soul, My Savior God, to Thee,
> How great Thou art, How great Thou art!

There they were, a ragtag group of riders in the middle of nowhere singing spontaneous praise to the God who created the wilderness they were exploring. The stark beauty of the terrain did what it was created to do: point God's creatures back to the glory of their Creator.

No one who was there will ever forget what happened that day. It was a remarkable event, maybe a once-in-a-lifetime occurrence.

But should experiences like this be rare? Yes, the scenery was extraordinary. Many will never see mountain glaciers and pristine wilderness. But still, God is always showing us His glory—in the Bible, in creation, and through our salvation— and responding with praise should be natural for Christians who catch sight of the glory of God. Theology should always result in doxology; the study of God should always lead to praise. To quote Sinclair Ferguson, 'The rhythm of the Christian's life is always determined by the principle that when the revelation of God in His glory is grasped by faith, the response is to return all glory to God.' [1]

---

1   Beeke, Joel R., *Living for God's Glory: An Introduction to Calvinism* (Orlando, FL: Reformation Trust Publishing 2008), 388.

Are you so caught up in the demands of everyday life, juggling the duties of home, school and work, that when you think about how to apply the theological truths you learn, your first thoughts are practical ones? Do you start with, 'What should I do? How can I serve? What items should I add to my to-do list?'

As we wrap up this study of God, the best first question to ask yourself is not 'What should I do?' but 'What should I sing?' What we do is certainly important, but our primary response to God's revelation of His glory should not be more action, but more praise. Hearts that sing go before hands that do.

Right before his plea for believers to live transformed lives in service to God, the apostle Paul wrote a song of praise:

> Oh, the depth of the riches and wisdom and knowledge of God!
> How unsearchable are his judgments and how inscrutable his ways!
>
> 'For who has known the mind of the Lord,
>   or who has been his counselor?'
> 'Or who has given a gift to him
>   that he might be repaid?'
>
> For from him and through him and to him are all things. To him
> be glory forever. Amen. (Rom. 11:33–36)

Paul wants us to pour out our lives in obedience to God—or, as he says elsewhere, to do everything for His glory—*because* we have seen the glory of God and our hearts are already bursting with praise to Him. 'To him be glory forever' is the reason for 'I appeal to you ... to present your bodies as a living sacrifice' (Rom. 11:33–12:2). Paul puts spontaneous singing before solemn service.

What is the rhythm of your life? The glorious God has shown Himself to you in His creation and in His Word. He has revealed His triune nature, His infinite attributes and His wondrous works. Have you returned all glory to Him? Have you begun to sing?

Appendix

ATHANASIAN CREED[1]

1. Whosoever will be saved, before all things it is necessary that he hold the catholic faith;
2. Which faith except every one do keep whole and undefiled, without doubt he shall perish everlastingly.
3. And the catholic faith is this: That we worship one God in Trinity, and Trinity in Unity;
4. Neither confounding the persons nor dividing the substance.
5. For there is one person of the Father, another of the Son, and another of the Holy Spirit.
6. But the Godhead of the Father, of the Son, and of the Holy Spirit is all one, the glory equal, the majesty coeternal.
7. Such as the Father is, such is the Son, and such is the Holy Spirit.
8. The Father uncreated, the Son uncreated, and the Holy Spirit uncreated.
9. The Father incomprehensible, the Son incomprehensible, and the Holy Spirit incomprehensible.
10. The Father eternal, the Son eternal, and the Holy Spirit eternal.
11. And yet they are not three eternals but one eternal.
12. As also there are not three uncreated nor three incomprehensible, but one uncreated and one incomprehensible.
13. So likewise the Father is almighty, the Son almighty, and the Holy Spirit almighty.

---

1   Accessed from https://www.ccel.org/creeds/athanasian.creed.html

14. And yet they are not three almighties, but one almighty.
15. So the Father is God, the Son is God, and the Holy Spirit is God;
16. And yet they are not three Gods, but one God.
17. So likewise the Father is Lord, the Son Lord, and the Holy Spirit Lord;
18. And yet they are not three Lords but one Lord.
19. For like as we are compelled by the Christian verity to acknowledge every Person by Himself to be God and Lord;
20. So are we forbidden by the catholic religion to say; There are three Gods or three Lords.
21. The Father is made of none, neither created nor begotten.
22. The Son is of the Father alone; not made nor created, but begotten.
23. The Holy Spirit is of the Father and of the Son; neither made, nor created, nor begotten, but proceeding.
24. So there is one Father, not three Fathers; one Son, not three Sons; one Holy Spirit, not three Holy Spirits.
25. And in this Trinity none is afore or after another; none is greater or less than another.
26. But the whole three persons are coeternal, and coequal.
27. So that in all things, as aforesaid, the Unity in Trinity and the Trinity in Unity is to be worshipped.
28. He therefore that will be saved must thus think of the Trinity.
29. Furthermore it is necessary to everlasting salvation that he also believe rightly the incarnation of our Lord Jesus Christ.
30. For the right faith is that we believe and confess that our Lord Jesus Christ, the Son of God, is God and man.
31. God of the substance of the Father, begotten before the worlds; and man of the substance of His mother, born in the world.
32. Perfect God and perfect man, of a reasonable soul and human flesh subsisting.
33. Equal to the Father as touching His Godhead, and inferior to the Father as touching His manhood.
34. Who, although He is God and man, yet He is not two, but one Christ.
35. One, not by conversion of the Godhead into flesh, but by taking

of that manhood into God.

36. One altogether, not by confusion of substance, but by unity of person.

37. For as the reasonable soul and flesh is one man, so God and man is one Christ;

38. Who suffered for our salvation, descended into hell, rose again the third day from the dead;

39. He ascended into heaven, He sits on the right hand of the Father, God Almighty;

40. From thence He shall come to judge the quick and the dead.

41. At whose coming all men shall rise again with their bodies;

42. And shall give account of their own works.

43. And they that have done good shall go into life everlasting and they that have done evil into everlasting fire.

44. This is the catholic faith, which except a man believe faithfully he cannot be saved.

NICENE CREED[2]

We believe in one God, the Father Almighty, Maker of heaven and earth, and of all things visible and invisible.

And in one Lord Jesus Christ, the only-begotten Son of God, begotten of the Father before all worlds; God of God, Light of Light, very God of very God; begotten, not made, being of one substance with the Father, by whom all things were made.

Who, for us men and for our salvation, came down from heaven, and was incarnate by the Holy Spirit of the virgin Mary, and was made man; and was crucified also for us under Pontius Pilate; He suffered and was buried; and the third day He rose again, according to the Scriptures; and ascended into heaven, and sits on the right hand of the Father; and He shall come again, with glory, to judge the quick and the dead; whose kingdom shall have no end.

And we believe in the Holy Ghost, the Lord and Giver of Life; who proceeds from the Father [and the Son]; who with the Father and the Son together is worshipped and glorified; who spoke by the prophets.

And we believe one holy catholic and apostolic Church. We acknowledge one baptism for the remission of sins; and we look for the resurrection of the dead, and the life of the world to come.

Amen.

---

2   Accessed from https://www.ccel.org/creeds/nicene.creed.html

Selected Bibliography

SYSTEMATIC THEOLOGIES

Berkhof, Louis. *Systematic Theology*. Grand Rapids, Michigan/ Cambridge, U.K.: Wm. B. Eerdmans Publishing 1996.

Calvin, John. *The Institutes of the Christian Religion*. Peabody, Massachusetts: Hendrickson Publishers, Inc. 2008.

Frame, John M. *Salvation Belongs to the Lord: An Introduction to Systematic Theology*. Phillipsburg, New Jersey: P & R Publishing 2006.

Grudem, Wayne. *Systematic Theology*: *An Introduction to Biblical Doctrine*. Leicester, England: Inter-Varsity Press and Grand Rapids Michigan: Zondervan 1994.

Horton, Michael. *The Christian Faith: A Systematic Theology for Pilgrims on the Way*. Grand Rapids, Michigan: Zondervan 2011.

Packer, J. I. *Concise Theology: A Guide to Historic Christian Beliefs*. Carol Stream, Illinois: Tyndale House Publishers, Inc., 1993.

Sproul, R. C. *Truths We Confess: A Layman's Guide to the Westminster Confession of Faith,* 3 Volume Set. Phillipsburg, New Jersey: P & R Publishing 2006.

BOOKS

Carson, D. A. *The God Who Is There: Finding Your Place in God's Story.* Grand Rapids, Michigan: Baker Books 2010.

Letham, Robert. *The Holy Trinity: In Scripture, History, Theology, and Worship.* Phillipsburg, New Jersey: P & R Publishing 2004.

Needham, N. R. *2000 Years of Christ's Power, Part One: The Age of the Early Church Fathers.* London, England: Grace Publications Trust 2011.

Packer, J. I. *18 Words: The Most Important Words You Will Ever Know.* Ross-shire, Scotland, UK: Christian Focus Publications 2007.

Packer, J. I. *Knowing God.* Downers Grove, Illinois: InterVarsity Press 1993.

Reeves, Michael. *Delighting in the Trinity*: *An Introduction to the Christian Faith.* Downers Grove, Illinois: IVP Academic 2012.

Sanders, Fred. *The Deep Things of God: How the Trinity Changes Everything.* Wheaton, Illinois: Crossway 2010.

White, James R. *The Forgotten Trinity: Recovering the Heart of Christian Belief.* Minneapolis, Minnesota: Bethany House Publishers 1998.

Wilkin, Jen. *None Like Him: 10 Ways God Is Different from Us (and Why That's a Good Thing).* Wheaton, Illinois: Crossway 2016.

E-books and Online Articles

'The Attributes of God—Chart.' http://www.preceptaustin.org/attributes_of_god.

Challies, Tim. 'Visual Theology—The Attributes of God.' https://www.challies.com/visual-theology/visual-theology-the-attributes-of-god/

Pink, A. W. *The Attributes of God.* https://www.monergism.com/attributes-god-ebook.

Sproul, R. C. 'The Attributes of God.' https://www.monergism.com/attributes-god-0.

Scripture Index

Christian Focus Publications

Our mission statement –

STAYING FAITHFUL

In dependence upon God we seek to impact the world through literature faithful to His infallible Word, the Bible. Our aim is to ensure that the Lord Jesus Christ is presented as the only hope to obtain forgiveness of sin, live a useful life and look forward to heaven with Him.

Our Books are published in four imprints:

CHRISTIAN FOCUS

popular works including biographies, commentaries, basic doctrine and Christian living.

CHRISTIAN HERITAGE

books representing some of the best material from the rich heritage of the church.

MENTOR

books written at a level suitable for Bible College and seminary students, pastors, and other serious readers. The imprint includes commentaries, doctrinal studies, examination of current issues and church history.

CF4•K

children's books for quality Bible teaching and for all age groups: Sunday school curriculum, puzzle and activity books; personal and family devotional titles, biographies and inspirational stories – Because you are never too young to know Jesus!

Christian Focus Publications Ltd,
Geanies House, Fearn, Ross-shire,
IV20 1TW, Scotland, United Kingdom.
www.christianfocus.com